Talking In Tones:

A Study Of Tone In Afro-European Creole Languages

Hubert Devonish

CARIBBEAN ACADEMIC PUBLICATIONS

Talking in Tones
A Study of Tone in Afro-European Creole Languages

First published in 1989 by
**Karia Press and
Caribbean Academic Publications**

Copyright © Hubert Devonish, 1989.
All rights reserved

Cover design by Hubert Devonish
Artwork by Maria Elias

ISBN 1 85465 006 8 Pb
ISBN 1 85465 007 6 Hb

Karia Press
41 Rheola Close,
London N17 9TR,
United Kingdom.

&

Caribbean Academic Publications
17 Valley Ridge, Cane Vale
Christ Church
Barbados

Printed and bound in Great Britain by
Biddles Ltd, Guildford and King's Lynn

only the second of these two rules applied historically. It acquired its long vowels not from intervocalic consonant deletion but through corrective pressure from English, the high status language with which it coexists.

Observation of the development of Guyanese Creole sheds some light on what may happen to demarcative stress in a tone language which undergoes syllabic restructuring of the type just discussed. Stress prominence previously associated with the syllable may become linked to the mora in the restructured language. This would have the effect of making such prominence tonal since mora prominence is, by definition, tonal.

Finally, in attempting to fit Afro-European Creole languages into a typology of tone languages, new features which serve to differentiate one type of tone language from another have come to light. Let us, for example, take the distinction which Hyman and Byarushengo (1984, p.89) make between languages with incomplete tonification and those not requiring any underlying tones to be specified at all. Our observation is that the relationship between H-tone and stress can play an important role in distinguishing between these two types of tone language. In a language such as Principense, where the syllable containing the H-toned mora is always stressed, the dissimilatory nature of stress blocks any assimilatory processes which H-tone might otherwise have been involved in. Such a language, therefore, does not require that any underlying tones be proposed. Rather, all that is necessary is information as to the mora in each word which would be marked for prominence. By contrast, an Afro-European Creole language such as Djuka only has stress associated with H-tone in certain environments. The absence of a permanent link between H-tone and stress occurs in a language with an H-tone which is able to take part in assimilatory processes. The existence of such processes requires that Djuka be regarded as an incompletely tonified language with underlyingly specified H-tones.

Chapter 1

On Locating Afro-European Creole Languages Within A Typology Of Prosodic Systems

1.0 Introduction

The acoustic feature, pitch, is associated with two distinct types of prosodic system in human languages. In languages with tonal systems, pitch is the sole acoustic cue employed in signalling the various tones which are used. In languages which have stress, pitch may be important, but is usually not the sole acoustic cue marking the distinction between stressed and unstressed syllables.

The tone-bearing unit in tone languages may be the syllable or the vowel depending on the language. In tonal languages, some or all of the tone-bearing units in a morpheme or word need to be specified in the lexicon as to their tonal identity, e.g. High, Mid, Low, etc. The abstract phonological category of tone receives its surface realization at the phonetic level by means of pitches which are high, mid, low, etc. relative to the pitch of other tone-bearing units in the environment. The significance of particular pitches in signalling tone does not lie in their absolute pitch heights. It lies rather in their pitch heights relative to the pitches of tone-bearing units in the immediate environment. This means that a particular pitch height may, in the same sentence of a given language, signal high tone and low tone at different points in the utterance. As an illustration of this, we need only refer to the many tone languages subject to intonational downdrift. In these languages, there is a gradual lowering in the general pitch levels of all tone-bearing units as the utterance proceeds, with the speaker maintaining the relative differences in pitch heights necessary to signal differences in tone.

Stress, a feature of the syllable, is often signalled by the presence of high pitch relative to the pitch of unstressed syllables in the environment. In fact, Lehiste (1970, p.125) among others, has made the strong claim that high pitch represents the most reliable cue for stress in European stress accent languages such as English. The problem is, therefore, how to distinguish between, on the one hand, high and low pitched syllables produced as a result of the presence or absence of stress, and, on the other, high and low pitched syllables produced as a result of the presence of High and Low tone. The solution lies in the fact that, unlike in the case of tone, pitch does not represent the only feature which may be associated with stress. There is loudness or intensity, traditionally considered as the primary marker of stress. Even though presently regarded as a less reliable indicator of stress than high pitch in certain languages, greater intensity is often associated with stressed syllables. This is the result of such syllables being produced with greater articulatory force. And, at the segmental level, there are other features associated with stress. Vowel lengthening tends to occur on short vowels in open syllables which are stressed. In addition, vowel reduction frequently takes place in unstressed syllables, often shifting vowel quality in the direction of schwa. Pike (1974) argues that these segmental effects associated with stress and lack of stress, are not linked to High and Low tone marking in tonal systems.

What, however, about the possibility of stress and tonal systems co-existing in the same language? On the question of the possible co-existence of a tonal system involving lexically-specified tone, and a stress system also involving the lexical specification of tone, there is some disagreement in the literature. Clements and Ford (1979, p.201) appear to believe that these two systems are mutually exclusive and never co-exist in the same language. On the other hand, Meussen (1970) lists some African languages investigated by other linguists, describing them as involving both lexically specified stress and tone. There is, however, some agreement that if such a co-existence of systems does occur, that such cases are relatively rare. Lea (1973, p.66) manages to straddle the two opposing positions by suggesting that if stress and tone contrasts both exist in a language at some point in its development, over time one type of contrast would become perceived as a contrast of the other type, depending on which is growing in importance. Far more common is the co-existence of fixed or predictable stress alongside a tonal system. One might well wonder what precisely are the phonetic cues for stress in such languages, in view of the fact that pitch would already be employed within the system of tone marking. In fact, however, pitch can still be used for signalling stress, as can be seen in the following example. According to Carter (1983, p.101), in the Eastern Bantu tone language, Tonga, a High tone immediately preceding a Low shows increased height, as in the example below. The low tone is unmarked in this example:

(1)   Níbákásíka   "When they arrived"

According to Carter, the syllable receiving stress in this manner also shows increased loudness. Stress reduction in Chinese results in an even wider range of surface level phonetic effects. Hyman (1975, p.208), in relation to the example which follows, points out that in the second syllable which is unstressed, the low back vowel /a/ is reduced to schwa, the voiceless /p/ is weakened to /b/, and the tone of

/pā/ is reduced to "neutral" tone which, in this case, is signalled by low pitch.

(2)   /lí pā/ -----> [lí bə]   "fence"

What, however, are the factors which can determine the location of predictable stress in tone languages? Carter (1983, p.101) points to two possible kinds of stress in these languages, positional stress and tone-related stress. Typical examples of the former are presented by the many Bantu languages which stress the penultimate syllable in the sentence or breath-group. An important phonetic feature of such stress is the lengthening of the stressed penultimate syllable, as cited by Carter (1983, p.100, p.106) for Bantu languages such as Shona, and illustrated in the examples in 5 below. In relation to tone-related stress, (1) above provides an example.

In addition to the influence which position and tone can exert in determining the location of predictable stress in tone languages, we need also to consider the role of syllable weight. In many non-tonal languages, syllables of the structure CVV or CVC, i.e. heavy syllables, receive stress in preference to light syllables, i.e. those with a CV structure. As we will see later on, the Creole tone languages, Saramaccan and Djuka, preferentially assign stress to heavy syllables of the CVV type.

There is one other kind of factor influencing the behaviour of stress in tone languages which we will consider here. In some languages, tone, usually High tone, operates as a mark of prominence, occurring only once within a word. Safwa, a Tanzanian Bantu language, is described by Voorhoeve (1973a) as having the location of prominence within the word determined partly within the lexicon and partly by phonological rule. Voorhoeve (1973a, p.1, fn.2) states that Safwa prominence includes both greater intensity and higher pitch. That prominence in this language is basically tonal as can be seen from the fact that the unit of prominence is the vowel or mora. In the examples below, involving prominent syllables with long or double vowels, prominence is assigned to different parts of the vocalic section of the syllable. In (3a), with the first part prominent, a High-Low or falling contour would be produced on the syllable. In (3b), a Low-High or rising contour would appear.

(3) a. íipa "here"
    b. iípo "there"

The fact that intensity becomes associated with the syllable containing the prominent vowel suggests that Safwa, as described by Voorhoeve, represents a language type in which stress is directly linked to the marking of prominence within the tonal system. Whenever a High-toned vowel appears, the syllable in which it occurs receives stress.

1.1 On Contact Between Stress Accent And Tonal Systems

In stress languages, English and Portuguese being two of this type, a lexical item is allowed to have no more than one stressed syllable. This is in marked contrast to multi-stress language systems such as those referred to by Pike (1974), which allow any or all syllables in a lexical item to receive stress. In a stress accent language such as English, with relatively free accent, the location of the stressed syllable is unpredictable, being largely determined within the lexicon. To the speaker of a tone language in which there is no stress, the high pitch associated with the stressed syllable in English would only be comparable to the High-tone within his own phonological system. One would, therefore, expect that any attempt to reproduce items of English origin within such a system, as for example in loan words, would result in High-tone being substituted for stress in the syllable which is accented in the source language. For speakers of tone languages which do have fixed, predictable stress, the situation would not be much different. The free, movable stress of the source language would be in no way comparable to the fixed stress of the receiving language. The unpredictable behaviour of the high-pitched, accented syllable in a stress accent language like English, could only bear comparison with the occurrence of High-tone. Here as well, the stressed syllable would be realised as High-tone within the phonological system of the receiving language.

In Yoruba, a tonal West African Kwa language, lexically determined stress is absent. In line with the hypothesis being put forward here, one would expect stress to become accommodated into the tonal system of Yoruba as High-tone in loan-words borrowed from a stress accent language such as English. This is borne out by the following examples taken from Salami (1972).

(4)   **Yoruba**   **English**

   a. kúù   <   'coup
   b. kóòmù   <   'comb
   c. grámà   <   'grammar
   d. sùkúrù   <   'school
   e. bɔ́tùlù   <   'bottle
   f. kɔ́bùrù   <   'corporal
   g. tìrìbúùnù   <   'tribune
   h. ɔposíʃǒn   <   oppo'sition

It would appear that, as in example (4)h, Mid-tone vowels are left unmarked in Salami's system of transcribing Yoruba. The selected examples serve only as an indicator of the dominant tendency in the adaptation of English loan-words. In a minority of loan-words from English, the location of High-tone is not predictable by reference to the place of the stressed syllable in the English original. In addition, more than one High-tone often occurs in English loan-words in Yoruba, and Mid-tones also occur. It is clear that a complex interaction takes place between the stress pattern of the originally English forms of many loan-words, and the tonal system of the borrowing language. Since, however, this rela-tionship is not the major focus of this work, we simply need here to note that the occurrence of stress in the original English forms of these loan-words coincides, in the vast majority of cases, with the position of a High-tone in the Yoruba forms.

The case of English loan-words in Shona, a Bantu language spoken in Zimbabwe, provides an even more interesting illustration of the way in which speakers of tonal languages associate the relatively free accentual stress of a language such as English, with High-tone. Shona is a language with fixed stress which falls on the penultimate syllable. The major cue for the presence of stress is vowel lengthening. In loan words of English origin, the penultimate stress of Shona remains constant, with the stress accented syllable of the original item being substituted for by High-tone. The examples which follow are taken from Carter (1983, p.106). The stressed syllables are underlined.

(5) a. [bhé:kà]   <   'baker
    b. [hwí:ndò]   <   'window
    c. [bhákì:ti]   <   'bucket
    d. [résì:pì]   <   'recipe
    e. [tébhù:rò]   <   'table
    f. [sìtókì:nzì] <   'stockings

As the examples from (5)c onwards make clear, there is a complete separation between the system of marking stress and that involved in the assigning of High-tone.

Further light can be shed on the nature of the outcome of contact between tonal and stress accent systems by examining the prosodic characteristics of a stress accent language as spoken by native speakers of a tone language. This represents a contrast with loan-word borrowing from a stress accent language into a tonal one. In the case of loan-word borrowing, the over-riding linguistic features are those of the receiving language, with the loans originating in stress accent languages providing the only non-native input. This allows us a chance to observe the nature of the interaction between the two types of prosodic system. A stress accent language as spoken by native speakers of a tone language provides us with another such opportunity to observe the interaction between systems. In this latter case, the dominant linguistic features would be those of the stress accent language, with the possibility, however, of tone-related interference from the speakers' first language.

Amayo (1980) suggests that in the area of the prosodic system, speakers of Nigerian English deviate considerably from the norms of metropolitan varieties of English. This is not simply a result of native language interference, but also stems from a nationalistic attitude towards Nigerian varieties of English on the part of its speakers. English is regarded as a Nigerian language variety, and it is, therefore, felt by many speakers that aspiring to the prosodic systems of metropolitan varieties of English is undesirable. Amayo, in examining standard and near-standard varieties of Nigerian English, hereafter simply referred to as Nigerian English, notes a tendency to substitute High-tone for stress, with syllables which are unstressed in other varieties of English receiving Low-tone. As part of the evidence that the high-pitch which appears on vowels of syllables in Nigerian English, and which would have been stressed in other varieties of English, represents tone rather than stress, he points to the nature of tone rules and the way they contrast with stress accent rules. Stress accent rules are entirely dissimilatory in character. The presence of stress on a particular syllable has the effect of making syllables in the immediate environment unstressed. In the case of tone rules, even though some of these may involve dissimilation, the vast majority tend to be assimilatory in nature, like the great bulk of phonological rules at the segmental level. Thus, in the tonal systems of many languages, a tone-bearing unit marked with High-tone would typically cause surrounding non-high tone-bearing units to assimilate and rise in pitch. (Hyman & Schuh, 1974, p.81).

Amayo (1980, p.7), in examining the Nigerian English speech of native-speakers of Yoruba, Edo and Hausa, first looks at the tone rules of each of these languages. In Yoruba, a High-tone following a Low-tone becomes a rise (ˇ). This results from a combination of Low followed by High on the same tone-bearing unit, creating a contour tone. Another Yoruba tone rule states that a Low-tone following a High-tone becomes a fall (^). Here, the fall comes about from a High-tone followed by a Low occurring on the same tone-bearing unit. Edo shares the second rule with Yoruba, but not the first. Hausa has neither of the two rules. The two rules could be represented as below.

(6) a. LH ----> L LH   (Yoruba)
    b. HL ----> H HL   (Yoruba, Edo)

In the examples which follow, we see the application or, where appropriate, the non-application of the rules in (6) to underlying High and Low tones in Yoruba, Edo and Hausa. The data is taken from Amayo (1980, p.5) and Hyman & Schuh (1974, p.90).

(7)
a. /òmíràn/   ---> [òmīrân]   "another one" (Yoruba)
b. /ókpè/   ---> [ókpê]   "flute"   (Edo)
c. /àlbárkà/ ---> [àlbárkà] "blessing"   (Hausa)

If Amayo's claim that High and Low tone are substituted for stress and lack of stress in Nigerian English is borne out, we would expect precisely the above kinds of rule to apply to the phonetic realization of tone in the English of Yoruba, Edo and Hausa speakers respectively. From the data which follows, it becomes clear that Nigerian English speakers not only convert English stress distinctions into tonal ones, but apply the tone rules of the first language to derive the surface phonetic realisations of these tones in their Nigerian English speech. This data is from Amayo (1980, p.6).

(8) English   Yoruba   Edo   Hausa

a. 'army   ármŷ   ármŷ   ármỳ
b. am'bition   àmbÝtîon   àmbítîon   àmbítiòn
c. exami'nation   èxàmìnátîon   èxàmìnátîon   èxàmìnátiòn

   From the above, it can be seen that speakers of Nigerian English with Yoruba as their first language, having converted stress and lack of stress into a High versus Low tone, apply rules (6)a & b of their native language to the surface realization of these tones. Edo speakers apply rule (6)b of their native language to their production of tones in their variety of Nigerian English. Native speakers of Hausa, to which neither of the two tone rules in (6) apply, produce on the surface level, the underlying tones derived from English stress, without modification.
   In the circumstances in which Afro-European Creole languages developed, whether in West Africa or the Americas, one would expect that a similar pattern of substituting High tone for stress would have emerged among the early contact vernaculars. The reasons for this expectation are simple. On the one hand, making up the vast majority of the newly emerging speech communities were people of West African origin, mainly native speakers of languages of the Niger-Congo language family. The great bulk of these languages can be considered tonal in the broadest sense of the term, i.e. employing tonal distinctions in a manner which can only be explained by the marking of items in the lexicon with some amount of tonal information. This is certainly true of the Kwa, Mande and Bantu sub-families. These are generally considered to have been the most important of the Niger-Congo languages involved in the emerging contact situations during the 17th and 18th centuries. The tonal information to be included in the lexicon may have involved the tonal specification of nearly every tone-bearing unit in the item, as would have been the case for Kwa languages such as Igbo and Yoruba. Or, this information may simply have related to the marking of parti-

cular entries as belonging to one of a restricted number of word-tone classes, as operates in some Mande and Bantu languages. Or, again, the lexical entry may have had to be marked simply for the tone-bearing unit within it, which contributes to a change in pitch level within the word or phrase, as is the case for Ijo, a Kwa language described as employing tonal accent by McCawley (1970). On the other side of the linguistic divide in the emerging Afro-European contact situations, were stress accent languages such as English and Portuguese. In the contact languages which emerged as lingua francas among the linguistically diverse African populations, the vast bulk of the vocabulary items were of European origin. It is reasonable to suppose that, amongst the African speakers of these emerging contact languages, sensitized as they were in their native languages to the linguistically significant use of tonal distinctions, High tone would have been substituted for stress in cases where the dominant source of vocabulary was either English or Portuguese.

Let us accept, for the time being, that the kind of stress-to-tone conversion suggested by the above discussion, did take place in the development of the early Afro-European contact language varieties. Modern-day Afro-European Creoles are distinct enough from the particular European sources of the bulk of their vocabulary, to be considered as separate languages. This distinctness exists at the lexico-semantic, syntactic and phonological levels, and is much greater than the difference between Nigerian English and British English. Thus, if substitution of tone for stress has occurred in Nigerian English, it is even more likely to have done so in the early stages of the development of these Creole languages. An acceptance of this assumption raises the question of what would have constituted the underlying tonal representations for items in these Proto-Creole languages. In a stress accent language, there would normally be a single stressed syllable per lexical item. Interpreted in tonal terms, this would mean one single tone-bearing unit marked for High tone per word, with the other units carrying Low tone. However, for speakers of languages such as Yoruba, in which the tonal identity of nearly every tone-bearing unit in an item needs to be specified within the lexicon, this predictability would not be immediately obvious. The result would be that such speakers would treat the emerging Proto-Creole as involving an opposition between underlying High and Low tones. The effect of this would have been the application of tone assimilation rules such as those in (6) a & b to tones in the new languages, as has occurred in comparable circumstances in Nigerian English.

What, however, of when speakers of the Proto-Creole languages become so familiar with the structure of their new language that they spot the generalisation that only one tone-bearing unit with High tone occurs per item? The effect of arriving at such a generalisation would be to change the nature of the underlying tonal representations which speakers have of items within the lexicon. Items would be marked for the tone-bearing unit which takes High tone, with the tonal identity of all other tone-bearing elements becoming redundantly specified, receiving Low tone at the surface level. In such circumstances, one would not expect tone assimilation rules of the sort presented in (6)a & b, since the underlying opposition is not between High tone and Low tone, but between High tone and zero specification. It is of significance to note that, in all the Creole languages investigated for this work, possessing a surprising variety of tonal rules, none seems to have tone assimilation rules such as (6)a & b.

The question then arises as to the stage at which speakers arrived at the above kind of generalisation. It is tempting to conclude that this most likely happened at the stage where the Proto-Creole moved from being a non-native language or "pidgin", to being the first language of speakers, becoming a true Creole language as the Niger-Congo languages fell into disuse among succeeding generations within the speech communities. However, Amayo (1980, pp.7-8) in a discussion of a similar development in Nigerian

English, provides evidence which would suggest that the shift from a High vs. Low contrast to one of High vs. Zero need not have awaited the appearance of native-speakers on the scene. According to Amayo, as some people's knowledge of Nigerian English improves, some or all of the phonological assimilation rules of the type presented in (6) and exemplified in (8) disappear. As a result, according to Amayo, it becomes more difficult to identify the mother tongue of speakers by way of their spoken English, even though their spoken English remains tonal. If the Nigerian English experience is anything to go by, the shift to a High vs. Zero tonal system may have occurred quite early in the development of Afro-European Creole languages, and well before the disappearance of native-speaker use of Niger-Congo tone languages within these speech communities.

1.2 On A Theoretical Framework For This Study

The theoretical approach of this study falls broadly within what has become known as autosegmental phonology. It was originally developed by Goldsmith (1976), and later applied by Haraguchi (1977) and Clements and Ford (1979) to the description of Japanese and Kikuyu respectively. It is based on the notion that tonal information and the segmental forms with which it becomes associated at the surface level, ought to be regarded as being quite separate at the underlying level. One of the tasks which the phonologist sets himself within this approach is to determine the rules, both language specific and universal, that associate the tonal tier with the segmental one at the surface level.
More specifically, this study will be relying on the concept of incomplete tonification first presented by Hyman (1982) and Hyman & Byarushengo (1984). According to this approach, there exists at one extreme, languages such as Yoruba and Igbo, generally regarded as "true" tone languages. Nearly every tone-bearing unit of every lexical entry in

these languages needs to be specified for their underlying tonal identity, i.e. High, Low, etc. However, even in a language such as Igbo, there are cases of tone-bearing units without tonal specification at the underlying level, and which end up receiving surface tonal realization by means of tone copying, usually from the preceding tone-bearing unit. Thus, in the Igbo examples below taken from Schuh (1978, p.234), the applicative extension with the form /rV/ (where V = preceding vowel), takes the surface tonal form High or Low, depending on the tonal environment which precedes. The extension, underlyingly toneless, is underlined in the examples.

(9) a. á nà m̀ èsírí yá nrí   "I'm cooking for him"
    b. ọ́ rùùrù há ọ́rụ́   "He worked for them"

However, there also exist languages, notably those of the Eastern Bantu group, which take the degree of incomplete tonification much further than is the case in Igbo. According to the analysis presented in Hyman (1982) and Hyman & Byarushengo (1984), languages such as these possess only one underlying tone, usually High tone, alongside gaps or zero specified units. It is this absence of tonal contrast at the underlying level which results in a marked difference in the nature of the tone rules in Eastern Bantu tone languages as compared with the tone languages of West Africa. The lack of underlying contrast between H and L tones among the latter set of languages results in there being no tonal assimilations of the sort presented for Yoruba and Edo in (6). As we have seen, and shall see later on, a similar absence of this type of tonal assimilation exists among Afro-European Creole languages, and for similar reasons.

McCawley (1978) argues, with particular reference to the Eastern Bantu languages Kikuyu, Luganda and Tonga, that there is no basis for creating a dichotomy between pure tone languages, on one hand, and pitch/tonal accent languages, on the other. He feels that the only validity for the dichotomy lies in it being applied to two stages in the derivation of a language. At the earlier stage, accentual rules operate resulting in accent reduction taking place, often at a considerable distance. Then, with pitch values assigned by rule to accented tone-bearing units, tone rules apply. McCawley (1978, p.128) states that the languages concerned differ from each other only in how deeply within their phonologies they become tonal. The proposals on incomplete tonification put forward by Hyman (1982) and Hyman & Byarushengo (1984), manage to capture McCawley's insight on the two stages while proposing a single unit, the underlying tone, as the participant in both stages of the derivation.

Taking the most common case in Eastern Bantu where the underlying tone is H, as in Haya, Luganda, Digo, etc., incomplete tonification allows us to explain the effects which H-tones are able to have on each other even when separated by several tone-bearing units. The explanation comes from the fact that intervening tone-bearing units are underlyingly zero-specified and do not, therefore, block the interaction between H-tones. Since only H-tones exist underlyingly, tonal assimilation between H's is not a possible phonological process. Dissimilation, however, is possible. It is this type of tone rule which, in traditional analyses of incompletely tonified languages, has been treated as accent reduction. With the interaction between underlying H-tones resolved, the next step is the assigning of tone to the specified tone-bearing units. In these languages, there are usually rules assigning H-tone to zero-specified units in certain specific environments, by means of tone copying from an underlying H-tone in the vicinity. Tone copying is clearly non-accentual in nature, as it involves an underlying H having an assimilatory effect on its environment, quite the opposite of the effect which a stressed syllable would have on neighbouring syllables in a stress accent language. In incompletely toni-fied languages of the kind being discussed, assimilation takes the form of tone copying rather than tone spreading of the type demonstrated in (6), because the affected environment has no tonal identity of its own.

Languages such as Yoruba and Igbo exist at one extreme on the scale of tonification. At the other extreme are languages such as Somali and Safwa. Although both of the latter languages employ tone at the surface level, there is no need to have tone represented at all at the underlying level. One tone-bearing unit per word carries High tone, with the others taking Low tone. The function of High tone in these languages is entirely of an accentual nature, akin to the role of stress in a stress accent language such as English. Somali and Safwa employ reduction or dissimilation rules, but no tone rules of an assimilatory nature. In these languages, one can truly be said to be observing tonal/pitch accent systems at work, as High tone functions purely as a marker of prominence for a given tone-bearing unit within a word. The unaccented tone-bearing units can be regarded as receiving Low tone by means of low-level detail rules. (Hyman and Byarushengo 1984, p.89).

Within this range of possible degrees of tonification, it will be interesting to see how the various Afro-European Creoles which exhibit tonal characteristics fit.

1.3 A Tonal Analysis Of Some Afro-European Creole Languages

1.31 Sranan

In Surinam, three Afro-English Creole languages are spoken - Saramaccan, Djuka and Sranan. Saramaccan is by far the most conservative of the three, all of which are considered by Alleyne (1980) to be more conservative than any of the other Afro-English Creole languages spoken in the Caribbean or West Africa.

Saramaccan owes its origins to the communities of Bush Negroes or runaway slaves set up in the forested areas of Surinam during the late 17th century. These slaves mainly escaped in the first twenty years of colonial settlement in Surinam which began in 1651. Surinam remained a British colony from its inception until the period around 1668, the year in which it finally passed to the Dutch. British influence rapidly declined with the bulk of the British settlers having left by 1680. Because of the newness of the plantation slave colony of Surinam, and the early stage at which the Saramaccan Bush Negroes fled, nearly all of these fugitives would have been born in West Africa and been native speakers of West African languages. Having been captured and transported to the Americas in a slave trade at that period dominated by the Portuguese, and in which the Portuguese-influenced contact language varieties were widely used, the original Saramaccan Bush Negroes would have had some exposure to Portuguese language influence. Finally, within the British dominated plantation society of early Surinam, they would have come into contact with English before they escaped to freedom. These facts serve to explain why, of a basic word list of 134 items whose origins are traceable, 72 are from English, 50 from Portuguese, and 6 are of African origin. (Voorhoeve, 1973b, p.138)

As for the African population who remained within Surinam plantation slave society, there was a chance for Afro-English contact to proceed much further, and for English to become an even more important source of lexical items. There was thus, by the beginning of the 18th century, two distinct but historically related Creole language varieties in Surinam. On one hand, there was Saramaccan, and on the other, Plantation Creole. An indication of the difference between these two varieties at that period can be seen by comparing the lexical sources of modern Sranan and Djuka, both originating in Plantation Creole, with the lexical sources of Saramaccan already presented above. Of a basic word list of 144 Djuka items whose origins are traceable, 116 are from English, 5 from Portuguese and 3 of African origin. Sranan presents a rather similar picture since, of 154 items, 118 are from English, 7 are from Portuguese, and 4 of African origin. (Voorhoeve, 1973b, p.138) It would appear from this evidence that, as Plantation Creole developed, items of English origin rapidly replaced those of Portuguese origin, as can be seen from (i) the great increase in the number of words of English origin, from 72 in Saramaccan to 116 and 118 in Djuka and Sranan respectively, and (ii) the decrease in the number of words of Portuguese origin, from 50 in Saramaccan, to 5 and 7 in Djuka and Sranan. Supporting evidence for the replacement of words of Portuguese origin by items of English origin is provided by Voorhoeve (1973b, p.139) when he deals with the significant number of Saramaccan synonyms of English and Portuguese origin. There are hardly any such synonyms in the basic vocabulary of Sranan. Interestingly enough, however, the originally English item in pairs of synonyms in Saramaccan is shared with Sranan. This suggests that the process of replacement of words of Portuguese origin by items from English already initiated in Saramaccan, was extended much further in Plantation Creole.

After the first decade of the 18th century, a new wave of marronage took place from the slave plantations of Surinam. These escapes and the establishment of new Bush Negro communities continued until the 1760's when peace treaties were signed by the colonial authorities with most of these groups. Escaping as they did, at a time when Plantation Creole was well established within the slave community, meant that it was this language, rather than any variety approximating to Saramaccan, which they took with them. These new Bush Negro communities continued to be in regular contact with plantation slave society via new escapees, raids and open visits in the period immediately after the signing of the peace treaties. However, according to Eersel (1984, p.6), by the late 1770's these Bush Negro groups were moving into isolation in the interior of Surinam for a period which was to last almost 200 years. It is this period which marks the separation between the variety of Plantation Creole spoken by the coastal slave population, on one hand, and that variety spoken by members of the Djuka, Saramaccan and Boni Bush Negro communities. The modern-day descendants of Plantation Creole are Sranan, spoken by the coastal population, and Djuka and related varieties, spoken by non-Saramaccan Bush Negroes.

Against this background, what is of great interest is that, whereas Saramaccan and Djuka have been described as tone languages (Glock, 1972; Huttar & Huttar, 1972; Voorhoeve, 1959, 1961), Sranan has been described by Hall (1948) as a stress accent language. By way of historical reconstruction, it would be logical to conclude that if Saramaccan, representing an earlier stage in the development of Plantation Creole is tonal, and if Djuka, one of the later developments of 18th century Plantation Creole too is tonal, then Plantation Creole was probably also tonal. One would, therefore, have to regard the development of a stress accent system in Sranan as an innovation. The question which arises is that of what set of linguistic changes could have triggered the shift from a system of tonal marking in 18th century Plantation Creole to that of stress accent in modern Sranan.

Based on written records of Plantation Creole as it was spoken in the 1770's in Surinam, Eersel (1984, p.4) concludes that the language as spoken at that time had a consonant-vowel (CV) syllable structure. Thus, all syllables normally consisted of no more than one consonant followed by a single vowel. The one partial exception seems to have involved the occurrence of the liquids /l/ and /r/ in certain lexical items, e.g. condre (Sr. kondre, "country"), macandra (Sr. makandra "together") and calcoo (Sr. krakun, "turkey"). In many other lexical items, however, consonant clusters involving liquids had not yet developed, e.g. masera (Sr. masra "master") and backera (Sr. bakra, "whiteman"). In a language such as this, with a CV syllable structure and employing a system of tonal marking, one could with equal justification propose that the tone-bearing unit was the syllable or the vowel. However, in the light of developments which subsequently took place in Djuka, and which we will examine in the discussion on Djuka in 1.3, it is most economical to treat the vowel as the tone-bearing unit in 18th century Surinam Plantation Creole.

In the latter part of the 18th century, Plantation Creole was coming under increasing influence from Dutch, the dominant European language in the society. One aspect of this influence took the form of an influx of new vocabulary items of Dutch origin. As Voorhoeve (1970, pp.63-64) points out, borrowings from Dutch into Sranan in its early formative period, i.e. the Plantation Creole stage, follow the pattern used for adapting words of English origin. However, later borrowings from Dutch allow the occurrence of diphthongs in closed syllables. This represents a clear modification of the Sranan syllable structure to accommodate Dutch borrowings containing diphthongs in their language of origin.

I would wish to propose, however, another aspect of the influence of Dutch on the syllabic structure of Plantation Creole as it developed into what is now Sranan. It was the effect of this particular form of influence which resulted in a shift from what was most likely a tonal system in Plantation Creole, to what is best described as a stress accent system in modern Sranan. Dutch is a language with a syllabic structure which allows consonant clusters in initial position, i.e. in the syllable onset, and syllable-finally, i.e. in the coda. The effect of pressure on a (C)(C)V(C)(C) language such as Dutch on a (C)V language like Plantation Creole would have been in the direction of the latter language altering its syllable structure rules to accommodate consonant clusters in the onset, and individual consonants as well as consonant clusters in the coda. In a stable, well-established language such as Plantation Creole was in the late 18th century, this type of syllabic restructuring could only take place by means of vowel deletions within the already existing vocabulary of the language. From the material cited above from Eersel (1984, p.4), this process was already beginning to take place in the 1770's in relation to certain words which did allow clusters involving a consonant and a liquid.

In order to understand how all this could have triggered off a shift from a tonal system to a stress accent system, we need to understand what the tonal system of Plantation Creole was, and the stress rules which operated within the language. We will here make an assumption that will be supported by evidence later. The assumption is that the tonal system of modern Djuka corresponds to that of 18th century Plantation Creole, except with regard to certain changes which have taken place in Djuka since the 18th century and which will be dealt with in the discussion of Djuka in 1.33. From the analysis of Djuka phonology presented by Huttar & Huttar (1972), and the Djuka lexical data in Huttar (1972), the underlying tonal system of Djuka, and by extension Plantation Creole, could be summed up as follows.

(10) The underlying tonal system in Modern Djuka/Surinam Plantation Creole

    a. Every lexical item has no more than one underlying H-tone, the location of this underlying tone on a specific tone-bearing unit (a vowel) being lexically determined.

    b. All other tone-bearing units are zero specified with those preceding the underlying H-tone being redundantly assigned L-tone, and those following receiving surface H-tone by way of tone copying. In the case of items in which no tone-bearing unit is associated with an underlying H, all tone-bearing units are redundantly assigned L-tone.

Stress in Djuka is predictable in relation to (i) syllable weight, i.e. syllables containing more than one vowel attract stress, (ii) the location of underlying H-tone, i.e. syllables containing a vowel associated with underlying H-tone receive stress in the absence of a heavy syllable, and (iii) position, i.e. in the event of no syllable in an item fulfilling the requirements of (i) or (ii), the penultimate syllable is stressed. (See Huttar & Huttar, 1972.) Since, as we shall see in 1.33 and 1.34, heavy syllables are a relatively recent development in Djuka as well as Saramaccan, it can be assumed that they did not exist in 18th century Surinam Plantation Creole. We can therefore reconstruct the stress assignment rules for Plantation Creole, based on those currently employed in Djuka, in the following way.

(11) Stress assignment rules for Surinam Plantation Creole

   a. Stress syllable containing the tone-bearing unit to which the underlying H-tone is lexically associated.

   b. Stress the penultimate syllable in items in which there is no underlying H-tone.

The vowels which were initially deleted as Plantation Creole evolved into modern Sranan, as Eersel (1984, p.4) demonstrates, were those occurring in interconsonantal position, one of the consonants in the environment being a liquid. Alleyne (1980, p.45, p.64) observes that these vowels had, before deletion, to have occurred in unstressed syllables. I would propose that this deletion of unstressed vowels, under continuing pressure from Dutch in the direction of a more complex syllabic structure, spread to a much wider range of environments. The major area of extension of the deletion process was to vowels in unstressed interconsonantal position, irrespective of whether either of the consonants was a liquid. In terms of stress assignment rule (11a), the syllables which were open to the deletion process were those which did not contain a vowel lexically associated with an underlying H-tone. Using items from Djuka as approximations of their original Plantation Creole forms, and their cognates from modern Sranan, we will observe the effect of the deletion process as it becomes introduced into what is now Sranan. The symbol ´ is used to mark underlying H-tone in the Djuka/Plantation Creole items, and stress in the Sranan equivalents. The data is taken from Huttar (1972).

(12) Djuka/Plantation   Sranan
      Creole

    a. bolón   > brón   "flour"
    b. wóluku   > wórku "cloud"
    c. béligi   > bérgi "mountain"
    d. kúsuwe   > kúswe "achiote"
    e. sinéki   > snéki "snake"
    f. sitáli   > stári "star"
    g. ákisi   > áksi   "ask"

In Djuka, lexical items without an underlying H-tone are rare, as presumably was the case for Plantation Creole. The result is that, in the sample Djuka word list of 351 items, no such item had a cognate in modern Sranan with a deleted vowel. As a result, we are unable to observe the effect which the stress assignment rule (11)b may have had on the development of consonant clusters as Plantation Creole developed into Sranan.

In spite of the process of deletion of vowels in unstressed syllables described above, such vowels do sometimes appear in modern Sranan, at least in certain lexical items. In fact, Alleyne (1980, p.65) refers to an observation made by Donicie and Voorhoeve (1963) that these vowels often occur in Sranan songs, so that *ston* "stone" may be sung as *siton*. Below are examples of occurrences of this vowel variability in certain lexical items taken from Hall (1948, pp.96-97).

(13)   a. néngere ~ néngre "negro"
        b. dómini ~ dómni   "priest"
        c. kápiten ~ kápten "captain"

d.	bigín	~	bgín	"begin"
e.	mamá	~	mmá	"mother"
f.	sipótu	~	spótu	"ridicule"
g.	bári	~	bár	"yell"
h.	aléysi	~	aléys	"rice"

In spite of the variability presented above, the dominant trend in modern Sranan is in the direction of vowel deletion in unstressed syllables and the creation of consonant clusters and closed syllables. In dealing with this phenomenon in Sranan, Alleyne (1980, p.65) states that "... a strong expiratory stress seems to have replaced high tone in Sranan... and induced loss of some unstressed vowels (syncope), thus creating consonant clusters and therefore, in some of these cases, consonant final syllables which do not exist in Saramaccan."

The position which is being taken in the present analysis is the direct opposite of Alleyne's. I am proposing that pressure from the phonological system of Dutch, the language with which Sranan has coexisted for over two centuries, has resulted in the development of a much more complex syllabic structure than the original (C)V structure of Plantation Creole. In order for this to occur, vowels had to be deleted. Vowels in unstressed syllables were naturally the prime target for this deletion process. However, the language into which these changes were being introduced was one which was not a stress accent language. It was instead a tonal one with incomplete tonification and stress which was predictable in relation to the location of the underlying H-tone.

In the syllable restructuring which took place in Sranan, stress moved from being a secondary feature associated with underlying H-tone to being a primary feature determining whether vowels in particular syllables could be deleted or not. Stress began to have a dissimilatory effect on syllables in the environment, therefore, allowing the deletion zero-specified vowels to which tone rules, notably tone copying, would otherwise have applied. By contrast with stress rules, tone rules are generally assimilatory in nature, as is, for example, the case with tone copying. In these circumstances, stress, a secondary feature associated with underlying H-tone prominence in Plantation Creole and Djuka, emerges as the dominant feature marking prominence in modern Sranan. Acoustically, no change takes place in the way that prominence is marked. The high pitch which was previously the major acoustic cue for H-tone, becomes perceived, along with intensity and the absence of vowel deletion, as a cue for stress. The change is one involving a transformation in the phonological behaviour of prominence as Surinam Plantation Creole developed into Sranan.

The effect on the Sranan lexicon of this shift in the system of marking prominence was that stress became applied to whichever syllable contained a vowel which was previously associated with underlying H-tone in Plantation Creole. This would have been quite a straightforward operation since, as Hall (1948, p.94) indicates, every syllable in Sranan contains no more than one vowel, with two successive vowels constituting two syllables. The examples in (12) above illustrate this conversion from tone to stress accent.

What, however, of those lexical items in Djuka and, by extension, Plantation Creole, with no underlying H-tone? Of the sample list of 341 Djuka items provided in Huttar (1972), only two lexical items were definitely identified as not possessing an underlying H-tone. These would be the items to which the Plantation Creole stress assignment rule (11)b would be expected to have applied. In the absence of an underlying H-tone, one would expect the predictable penultimate stress of Djuka/Plantation Creole to be converted into the stress accent of Sranan. The first of the two items, a monosyllabic word, is not very useful in helping to establish what the process was in these cases since there is only one syllable on which to apply stress accent in Sranan. The second, consisting of three syllables, suggests that penultimate stress in Plantation Creole was indeed converted to stress accent in Sranan. However, the fact that we are able to present only one such case makes such a conclusion very tentative indeed.

(14)   Djuka/Plantation   Sranan
        Creole

    a.   daai   >   dráj   "turn"
    b.   aboma   >   abóma   "boa"

We have attempted here to establish that Surinam Plantation Creole was a tonal language with incomplete tonification involving an opposition between the vowel, if any, directly associated with the underlying H-tone, and the zero-specified vowels whose tonal form on the surface was predictable. The syllable with the vowel associated with the underlying H-tone, received stress. When syllabic restructuring induced by pressure from Dutch resulted in the deletion of many vowels in unstressed syllables, stress emerged as the dominant feature of prominence in what had, up to then, been a tonal system with stress predictable from the tonal environment. It is, in this fashion, that the stress accent system of modern Sranan probably emerged.

1.32 Principense

Principense is a Creole language with a lexicon predominantly of Portuguese origin. It is spoken in the island of Principe, presently part of the Republic of Sâo Tomé and Principe in the Gulf of Guinea off the West African Coast. It is basically a language with a (C)V syllable structure, i.e. syllables are made up of no more than one consonant followed by an obligatory vowel. However, due to pressure from Portuguese, the official and high prestige language with which it coexists, more complex syllable structures have become possible in Principense. This is an issue which we shall return to later.

According to Traill and Ferraz (1981, p.208), Principense has a system of marking prominence in lexical items which involves either (i) high pitch, (ii) high pitch and intensity, or (iii) high pitch, intensity and slight vowel lengthening. The linguistic facts as presented up to now are quite consistent with an analysis of Principense as a language employing a stress accent system. This would be consistent with the position already taken in 1.1 that high pitch is often the most reliable acoustic cue for the presence of stress. However, whereas high pitch as a marker of stress is associated with the entire syllable to be marked for prominence, high pitch as a marker of prominence in Principense is associated with the vowel. Evidence for this comes from the fact that the language has, in the course of its evolution, developed syllables composed of two vowels, i.e. a CVV syllable structure, in which either vowel could receive prominence. The result is a falling tone on the syllable when the first vowel is marked for prominence, and a rising tone when the second vowel is involved.

In order to better understand the nature of the prosodic system of modern Principense, it may be useful to trace the way in which this system emerged and developed. Historical reconstructions of early Afro-European Creole languages such as that done by Alleyne (1980), coupled with an analysis of the phonological adaptation which has taken place in the absorption of words of Portuguese origin into Principense (Valkhoff, 1966, pp.89-92; Ferraz, 1975, pp.154-161), would suggest a CV syllable structure for early Principense. In addition, evidence from modern Principense would indicate that it was a tone language with incomplete tonification, involving an opposition between H-tone vs. zero at the underlying level, with the location of the H-tone usually corresponding with that of the stressed syllable in Portuguese cognates. Some examples from modern Principense taken from Ferraz (1975) and Traill and Ferraz (1981) serve as illustrations of the kind of syllabic and prosodic modifications applied to words of Portuguese origin entering Principense.

(15)   Principense   Portuguese

   a.   rέzi   <   'raiz   "root"
   b.   désu   <   'Deus   "God"
   c.   vedádi   <   ver'dade   "truth"
   d.   kɔnéta   <   cor'neta   "horn"
   e.   ɔ́zɛgɛ   <   'osga   "gecko"
   f.   kálima   <   'calma   "calm"
   g.   firíya   <   'fria   "cold"

The modifications which take place above at the segmental level involve the adaptation of words of Portuguese origin to the basic CV syllabic structure of Principense by (i) deletion of a final consonant in a closed syllable as in (15)c and d, (ii) creation of an additional syllable by the introduction of a vowel in environments where the CV structure would otherwise be violated as in (15)a and b. At the prosodic level, the stressed syllable of the Portuguese cognates corresponds to the location of H-tone in Principense items.

Traill and Ferraz (1981, pp.211-214) describe a phenomenon in which "...a CVCV structure is produced through reduction in the number of syllables or apparent deletion of certain consonants in an initial or medial cluster..." in words absorbed into Principense from Portuguese. The consonant involved in the process is, in all cases cited, a liquid, and one of the syllables involved is always one which takes stress in Portuguese. The analysis of this process has to begin with the assumption that vowel insertion originally took place to break up all such consonant clusters in which the liquid is part of the stressed syllable in Portuguese. Since H-tone would have been functioning as a substitute in Principense for Portuguese stress accent, one of the two syllables involved would always have been H-toned in Principense.

The question now arises, however, of what historically could have triggered the deletions of such inter-vocalic liquids, giving rise to the possibility of CVV syllables in the language. The answer lies in the continuing influence on Principense of Portuguese, a language with which it has co-existed from the time of the original Afro-European contact situation in the 16th century. Portuguese, a language which allows certain syllable-initial consonant clusters as well as closed syllables, would have been exerting a general pressure on Principense in the direction of a more complex syllable structure. Inter-vocalic liquid deletion resulting in the creation of long or heavy syllables would represent a shift in this general direction while not compromising the principle of the language not allowing initial consonant clusters or closed syllables. Since stress (intensity) is predictable in Principense in relation to H-tone, occurring on the syllable containing the H-toned vowel, the presence of stress is likely to have been the determining factor in setting off the liquid deletion. As has already been established, it is stress, not H-tone, which has effects at the segmental level in human languages. It is quite normal for stress to lengthen vowels and even cause them to diphthongise as occurs in Italian. (Hyman, 1975, p.208) The fact that a liquid deletion rule creating heavy syllables seems to have applied only in the environment of a stressed syllable, i.e. one containing an H-toned vowel, points to stress as the determining factor. Generally in languages, stress tends to be attracted to heavy syllables. In Principense, stress seems to have been involved in liquid weakening rather than the more normally observed process of vowel weakening as was seen, for example, in our discussion on Sranan. In so doing, a syllable-type more favourable to bearing stress has been created.

In (16) below, is an attempt to represent the process by which items containing a syllable with a long vowel may have developed in Principense from their Portuguese cognates. The Portuguese forms are marked for stress. The intermediate forms, representing an earlier phase in the development of Principense are marked for both stress and H-tone, as are the forms from modern Principense.

(16) Portuguese   Early   Modern
                    Principense   Principense

   a. 'fruta   >   fu'rúta   >   'fuúta   "bread-fruit"
   b. 'furta   >   'fúruta   >   'fúuta   "steal"
   c. 'preto   >   pe'rétu   >   'peétu   "black"
   d. 'perto   >   'péretu   >   'péetu   "near"
   e. a'braço   >   ba'rásu   >   'baásu   "embrace"
   f. 'serve   >   'sírivi   >   'síivi   "serve"
   g. ba'rata   >   ba'ráta   >   'baáta   "cheap"
   h. ca'roço   >   ko'rósu   >   'koósu   "pip"

Justification for the proposition that an epenthetic vowel existed in Early Principense in the cases of examples (a)-(f) above, can be found in Modern Principense in the form of examples such as firíya "cold" from Portuguese 'fria cited in (15)g. The examples above would suggest that (i) stress in the two Principense varieties remained associated with the syllable containing the vowel in the stressed syllable of the Portuguese cognate, and (ii) H-tone in the Principense varieties was linked to the vowel found in the stressed syllable of the Portuguese cognate. The effect of inter-vocalic liquid deletion in Modern Principense is to produce stressed syllables with long vowels, with rising or falling tones on such vowels depending on whether it was the first or second vowel which was H-toned in the earlier phase of the language.

The syllable structure restrictions blocking syllable-initial consonant clusters and closed syllables are no longer active in Modern Principense. As a result, the original motivation behind inter-vocalic liquid deletion, i.e. the creation of a more complex syllable structure while not violating these restrictions, has disappeared. Traill and Ferraz (1981, pp.213-214n) attribute the modification in syllable structure to the great degree of influence from Portuguese to which Principense has been subjected since the beginning of the 20th century. The result is that syllable-initial consonant clusters involving a liquid as a second member, as well as syllables closed by liquids do occur as in the examples below taken from Traill and Ferraz (1981). Particularly interesting is the case of (17)a in which the sequence /trí/ varies with /tíi/ in a lexical item in Modern Principense. In terms of the analysis being presented here, the latter sequence would be derived historically from /tirí/ as in the examples in (16). The former sequence, on the other hand, would be considered to have been introduced more recently as a result of much more direct influence from Portuguese.

(17) a. trígu ~ tiígu   "wheat"
      b. ladró   "thief"
      c. strétu   "narrow"
      d. árbe   "weed"

Principense operates an accentual system. Each item needs to be specified in the lexicon for the location of accent. The unit which is marked for prominence in Principense is the vowel. As a result, fuúta "breadfruit" and peétu "black" are distinguished from fúuta "steal" and péetu "near". Stress is associated in Principense with the syllable containing the vowel marked for H-tone, which would result in the first syllable of both minimal pairs being stressed. The distinction, therefore, clearly is not one of stress. Rather, what is involved is the location of high pitch within the syllable itself, occurring on the first or second vowel, and creating a rising or falling pitch contour over the entire syllable. The fact that the domain of prominence is the vowel suggests that Principense is a pitch or tonal accent language, with each item needing to be lexically specified as to the vowel which will receive prominence by means of high pitch.

Even though the domain of prominence in Principense is the vowel, in contrast to Sranan in which it is the syllable which is accented, the difference between the prosodic systems of these two Afro-European Creole languages is one of degree rather than of kind. In Principense, the fact that in syllables with long vowels, one of the two vowels is always H-toned, suggests that stress and the surface manifestation of H-tone have become inseparable. The reason for this conclusion is that if the two were separable, the language would have allowed the development of syllables with long vowels containing only L-toned vowels. In such an event, the heavy syllable, i.e. that containing the long vowel, would have received stress in preference to the syllable with the H-toned vowel. As has been well established, stress is essentially dissimilatory in nature. With the inseparable association between stress and H-tone in Principense, one would not expect such a H-tone to be involved in the assimilatory rules which tones generally participate in. The evidence provided by Traill and Ferraz (1981) seems to support this in that only one surface H-toned vowel seems able to occur in any item in the language. Like in the case of Sranan, therefore, it would be incorrect to propose the existence of an underlying H vs. zero tonal distinction. Rather, what is necessary for Principense is simply a mark of prominence assigned to the vowel, and realised on the surface in the form of high pitch.

Evidence that Principense, under the continued influence of Portuguese, may be heading in the direction of a stress accent system such as that of Sranan can be seen from the examples in (17). Examples (b)-(e) all represent cases where, if the CV syllable were still the only acceptable syllable structure in the language, and if inter-vocalic liquid deletion were still active, syllables with long vowels would have been created. Example (a) represents a case where a form with a long vowel is being replaced by one with a liquid followed by a short vowel, under the influence of Portuguese syllable structure rules. The disappearance of long vowels would produce a system of marking prominence based on the syllable, and in which high pitch and stress would always coincide. Such a system would be identical to the stress accent system of Sranan.

1.33 Djuka

Djuka, a Surinam Bush Negro English-lexicon Creole language already referred to in 1.31, is a language with a prosodic system which is best described in terms of incomplete tonification. Every lexical item, i.e. those items which are not clitics or affixes, must be marked within the lexicon for the tone-bearing unit if any, to be associated with an underlying H-tone. Such a tone-bearing unit is marked as prominent by this association, since there is normally a maximum of one such tone-bearing unit per lexical item. What is involved in Djuka is more than the use of high pitch to signal vowel rather than syllable prominence in a manner similar to Principense. This can be seen from the fact that the H-tone involved in marking prominence in Djuka takes part in tone rules, most notably tone copying.

The tone copying just referred to involves the underlying H-tone copying on to all the tone-bearing units within the lexical item which follow the unit with which the H-tone is lexically associated. The tone-bearing units preceding that lexically associated with the underlying H-tone are redundantly assigned L-tone by low level detail rules. In (18), an attempt is made to illustrate how this operates. The unbroken line represents the link between the underlying H-tone and the tone-bearing unit with which that tone is initially associated. The broken lines represent, on the other hand, the association of untoned units with surface tone by means of either (i) tone copying, or (ii) low level detail rules.

(18)

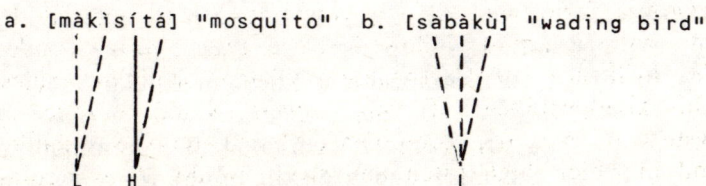

a. [màkìsítá] "mosquito"   b. [sàbàkù] "wading bird"

In (19) below, we have before us a set of examples

taken from Huttar & Huttar (1972) and Huttar (1972). They are presented in a form which is intended to demonstrate how, via the tone assignment rules illustrated in (18), speakers of Djuka move from underlying forms in which at most the location of a single H-tone is specified, to surface forms in which every tone-bearing unit is marked for tone. In addition, it becomes quite clear, particularly from examples (c) and (d), that the tone-bearing unit in Djuka is the vowel. In these examples each involving syllables with two vowels, the underlying H-tone is associated with the first vowel in the case of (c) and the second in (d).

(19) a. /búku/   ---- [búkú]   "book"
      b. /buku/   ---- [bùkù]   "fungus"
      c. /páati/   ---- [páátí]   "priest"
      d. /baáka/   ---- [bàáká]   "black"
      e. /ákisi/   ---- [ákísí]   "ask"
      f. /somóko/   ---- [sòmókó]   "smoke"
      g. /kosubéi/   ---- [kòsùbéí] "near"

In Djuka, there are two basic syllable types which need to be distinguished. On one hand, there are light syllables possessing a CV(N) structure and composed of just one vowel. Such syllables are treated as constituting single moras in the process of stress assignment in the language. On the other hand, there are heavy syllables. These have a CVV(V)(N) structure and, with a minimum of two vowels involved, count as two moras in stress assignment. A reinterpretation of the analysis presented by Huttar & Huttar (1972) would provide the following rules governing the composition of the stress foot in Djuka.

(20) Stress foot composition rules for Djuka

   a. A stress foot is composed of a minimum of one mora and a maximum of four, with no more than one heavy syllable occurring per stress foot.

    b. A heavy syllable is blocked from occurring foot-initially in a foot with four moras.

A lexical item, i.e. any morpheme which is neither a clitic nor an affix, belongs to at least one stress foot in Djuka. Such an item contains, as a result, at least one stressed syllable. The issue of whether a given lexical item belongs to one or more stress feet is determined by the extent to which the segmental shape of the item corresponds to the restrictions placed on what can occur in a stress foot. In cases where such restrictions are violated, the item is assigned to two separate stress feet, thus receiving two stresses. In (21) is presented an adaptation of the stress assignment rules for Djuka as proposed by Huttar & Huttar (1972, p.6)

(21) Djuka stress assignment rules

    a. If a foot contains a heavy syllable, that syllable is stressed.

    b. In the absence of a heavy syllable, the syllable containing the vowel with the underlying H-tone is stressed.

    c. If neither heavy syllable nor underlying H-tone exists within the foot, the penultimate syllable receives stress.

    d. The only syllable in a monosyllabic foot is stressed by definition.

As has been mentioned 1.31, heavy syllables are a relatively new feature in Djuka, having developed some time after the isolation of Djuka speakers from speakers of Coastal Plantation Creole. This took place in the late 18th century. I would suggest, as has already been done for Principense, that the influence of the dominant European language, Dutch in this case, was responsible for this development in what was previously a language with a simple CV(N) syllable structure. Dutch, like Portuguese, is a language which permits certain syllable-initial consonant clusters. In addition, it allows closed syllables ending in consonants other than nasals. Djuka would have been under a degree of influence from Dutch to allow for the inclusion of a greater amount of segmental information within the syllable. A more direct source of influence would have come from Sranan which many Djuka speakers employ as a second language. Sranan itself, under the influence of Dutch, has modified its syllable structure to accommodate initial clusters and syllables closed by non-nasal consonants.

If Djuka speakers attempted to accommodate to pressure for a more complex syllable structure, while continuing to block syllable-initial consonant clusters and syllables closed by non-nasal consonants, the development of heavy syllables with more than one vowel would seem to be the logical outcome. One major source of such syllables involves the deletion of liquids which originally occurred inter-vocalically. In (22) below, we see reconstructed Plantation Creole forms with a CVLV sequence, the Sranan forms which in (e) - (h) have one of the vowels deleted to produce a single syllable, and the Djuka forms with inter-vocalic liquid deletion producing the same effect.

(22)
	Plantation Creole	Sranan	Djuka	
a.	*tyári	tyári	tyái	"carry"
b.	*fúlu	fúru	fúu	"full"
c.	*béle	bére	bée	"belly"
d.	*dólo	dóro	dóo	"door"
e.	*dilíngi	dríngi	diíngi	"drink"
f.	*sikilífi	skrífi	skiífi	"write"
g.	*kolósi	krósi	koósi	"clothing"
h.	*kalábu	krábu	kaábu	"crab"

The application of the historical inter-vocalic liquid deletion rule has been idiosyncratic, leaving such liquids intact in many lexical items, as in the examples cited in (12)a, b, c, and f. There is a greater likelihood of the liquid deletion having taken place in cases where the first and second vowels are the same, but (22)a <u>tvái</u> is an example of liquid deletion having taken place in an environment where the two vowels were not the same. A glance at the above examples coupled with the knowledge that stress, in the absence of a heavy syllable, is assigned to the syllable containing the vowel with the underlying H-tone, leads one to the following conclusion. What occurred historically in Djuka was a stress induced vowel strengthening by means of inter-vocalic liquid deletion. This would suggest some similarity between the processes of marking prominence in Djuka and Principense where a comparable historical development has taken place. If the two languages have developed along such similar lines, how is it then that we propose for Djuka incomplete tonification with an underlying H-tone, but simply vowel-based prominence for Principense with no underlying H-tone?

The answer to this question lies in the area of the precise relationship which existed between stress and tonal prominence prior to the development of heavy syllables in the two languages. An examination of the stress assignment rules for Djuka in (21) would show that stress can be assigned in a stress foot which contains neither a heavy syllable nor a syllable with a H-toned vowel. According to (21)c and d, in such circumstances stress is assigned to the penultimate syllable or to the only syllable in a monosyllabic foot. These stress assignment rules, applying as they do in stress feet without heavy syllables, are very likely to have existed prior to the development of such syllables in Djuka. What this implies is that prominence marked by underlying H-tone and stress prominence were and continue to be quite separate and distinct phenomena. Before the development of heavy syllables in the language, these two phenomena happened to coincide in stress feet in which there was an underlying H-tone. In the modern language, they coincide if the H-tone is present and there is no heavy syllable. In Principense, however, from the information provided by Traill and Ferraz (1981), stress invariably is only applied to syllables containing a vowel with H-tone. As a result of this difference between the two languages, H-tone in Principense is purely a vowel based marker of prominence coinciding with stress, whereas, in Djuka, one is dealing with an H-tone which is more than a marker of prominence. Djuka H-tone, because of its independence from stress, can be involved in processes such as tone copying which characterize underlying tones in languages with incomplete tonification.

In spite of the independence of stress from underlying H-tone in Djuka, a shift in the location of stress resulting from the development of the heavy syllable has triggered off a shift in the position of underlying H-tone in many lexical items. In these cases, an underlying H-tone was associated with a vowel in a syllable which was consequently stressed in Plantation Creole.

With the development of a heavy syllable within the same stress foot as Djuka, underlying H-tone has moved to the first vowel of the newly created heavy syllable thus following the shift in stress. If this process had been uniformly applied across all lexical items with heavy syllables in the language, it may have become necessary to describe Djuka as a stress accent language with a distinction between light and heavy syllables, marking prominence by means of a combination of high pitch and intensity. Below are some examples of stress induced tone shift in modern Djuka taken from Huttar (1972).

(23) | | Plantation Creole | Sranan | Djuka | |
|---|---|---|---|---|
| a. | *bósoro | bósro | bosóo | "brush" |
| b. | *nángara | nángra | nangáa | "claw" |
| c. | *kóndere | kóndre | kondée | "country" |
| d. | *óndoro | óndro | ondóo | "hundred" |
| e. | *wátara | wátra | watáa | "water" |

f.	*filíngi	fríngi	fíingi	"throw"
g.	*kakaláka	kakaláka	kakáaka	"cockroach"

As has been established in the preceding discussion, Djuka can be described as a language with incomplete tonification involving an underlying H-tone vs. zero opposition. At the surface level, however, every tone bearing unit bears either an H or L tone. This comes about via tone copying in the case of zero-specified tone-bearing units with a surface H-tone, or by low-level detail rules in units with surface L-tone. Justification for maintaining a distinction between underlying tonal representation and surface tone can be seen in the operation of certain tone rules which apply exclusively to surface tone. In the case of one such rule, a L-H sequence across a syllable boundary becomes H-L in an environment preceding one or more low tones followed by final pause with no underlying H-tones in an intervening foot. However, a subsequent syllable in the same foot may be H-toned. (Huttar & Huttar, 1972, p.7) Thus, the item /tabíki/ "island" becomes [tábìkí] in the sentence in (24).

(24) [pyá tábìkí dè] "Where is the island?"

In the rule to represent this change presented in (25), the symbol $ stands for syllable boundary, / for stress foot boundary, and // for final pause.

(25) L $ H > H $ L / $\cdots$ H$_o^n$ / L //

The above rule has to be regarded as applying to surface rather than underlying tones. The vowel in the syllable /-ki/ must have received its surface tone from the underlying tone of the vowel in /-bi-/ by way of tone copying before the tonal metathesis took place. Otherwise, how would one explain the presence of H-tone on /-ki/? In addition, the fact that the H-tone on the vowel in /ta-/ fails to copy on to the second vowel of the surface form, suggests that the H-tone involved here is not the underlying

H-tone but a surface tone. Along similar lines, the fact that the second vowel receives L-tone suggests that this is the tone assigned to /ta-/ by low level detail rules, and that rule (26) applies only after such rules have operated.

Djuka appears to be an Afro-European Creole language which has developed a system of tonal prominence as a result of the interaction between Niger-Congo tonal systems and stress accent systems of English and, to a lesser extent, Dutch. More than simply being a vowel based system of marking prominence, the tonal system of Djuka has to be regarded as one in which there is a limited degree of tonification involving an underlying H-tone. The location of this underlying H-tone usually coincides with the placement of stress in cognate items in English, Dutch, etc. However, a certain number of internally motivated tone changes have taken place which result in shift in the location of the underlying H-tone, destroying the correspondences with the location of stress in European cognate items, as in nearly all the words in (23).

1.34 Saramaccan

Voorhoeve (1961b, pp.151-156) argues that, in Saramaccan, there is a special category of word which has no lexical significance of its own, never occurs in isolation and is used to signal intensity. In his view, such words, ending as they do with two or more H-toned vowels, deviate from the normal tonal structure of words in the language. Another category of word involved in such deviation is onomatopoeia. The discussion of the tonal system of Saramaccan which follows will ignore these exceptional cases.

Every lexical item, i.e. those items which are not clitics or affixes, is composed of one or more stress feet, according to Rountree (1972, p.22). This would, of course, mean that every such item would contain at least one stressed syllable. Non-compound lexical items may contain one stress foot, as in

(26)a & b below, or more than one as in c & d. There are also compound lexical items. These are composed of the stress feet associated with the individual items which make them up, as can be seen in e & f. Finally, as in g & h, lexical items can combine with affixes and clitics. These latter items have no stress of their own. Phonological feet in Saramaccan can be seen, therefore, to correspond to simple lexical items, parts of such items or to lexical items with affixes and clitics. The symbol / in the examples marks the boundary between two stress feet.

(26)
a. wáka   "walk"
b. haíka   "listen"
c. sikí/si   "six"
d. kalu/wá   "lizard"
e. líba/-se   "upriver"
f. gan/-gádu   "the great god"
g. ta-woóko   "working"
h. sí-de   "see there"

The rules for assigning stress to the appropriate syllable within the stress foot are presented in (27) as adapted from Rountree (1972, pp. 25-26).

(27) Saramaccan stress assignment rules

a. The first heavy syllable is stressed.

b. In the absence of a heavy syllable within the foot, the penultimate syllable receives stress.

c. In two-syllable lexical items with the underlying H-tone associated with a tone-bearing unit in the second syllable, stress may variably be assigned as in (b) or to the final syllable, i.e. the one containing the vowel associated with the underlying H-tone.

If one were to adopt the position taken by Rountree

(1972, p.25) and regard the word stem as the basic unit within which the tonal system operates, one would end up concluding that there are three different types of tonal pattern possible in Saramaccan. The most frequently occurring pattern would be that in which only one tone-bearing unit within the stem is lexically associated with an underlying H-tone. Less frequent would be those stems with no tone-bearing unit which has a lexical association with an underlying H-tone. Even rarer would be those items with more than one tone-bearing unit having a lexical association with underlying H-tones. The existence of the last of these three possibilities, regardless of how rare such stems may be, would make it difficult to argue that underlying H-tone operates as a marker of prominence in Saramaccan. The other two tonal patterns are, of course, consistent with an analysis of underlying H-tone as marking prominence. The very frequency with which these occur coupled with the rarity of the third tone pattern, tend to point in the direction of an analysis involving tonal prominence. The problem would be one of how to deal with the cases of word stems with more than one underlying H-tone.

The solution being proposed here involves regarding the stress foot rather than the word stem as the basic unit within which the tonal system operates. According to this analysis, every stress foot would contain at most a single tone-bearing unit having an association with an underlying H-tone. Excluded from this account of the tonal facts of Saramaccan are, of course, words of intensification and onomatopoeia which, as we have already pointed out, deviate from the normal tone structure of items in the language. This account of the tonal system of Saramaccan would require (i) that every word stem be specified in the lexicon as to the boundaries between stress feet where the stem is made up of more than one foot, and (ii) that every stress foot be specified as to the location of the tone-bearing unit, if any, which is associated with an underlying H-tone. The first of these requirements is in any case implied by Rountree

(1972, p.25) who presents examples such as (26) c & d. In these examples, the presence of two stress feet rather than one, along with the location of boundaries between them, cannot be predicted by reference to any feature within the phonological structure of the words. Requirement (ii), in conjunction with requirement (i), has the effect of treating simple lexical items with more than one stress in the same fashion as compound items. In compound items such as (26)e, the compound parts, independent morphemes in their own right, retain their individual stresses and separate tonal identities. The parallel with non-compound items containing two stress feet is obvious, the only difference lying in the lexical status of the phonological sequences making up the individual feet.

Support for this approach can be found in Voorhoeve (1961b, pp.153-156). This support takes two forms. Firstly, he points out that at least in the case of some lexical items with two underlying H-tones, one is dealing with forms which were originally compounds but which are no longer perceived as such because the individual morphemes have fallen out of use. Such an explanation could just as well apply to lexical items with one or no H-tone but which belong to stress feet. Secondly, the tone rules which he presents for Saramaccan operate across boundaries between stress feet, regardless of whether these boundaries coincide with morpheme or word boundaries or not. It is the operation of these tone rules which we will now investigate.

Every tone-bearing unit not associated with an underlying H-tone is redundantly assigned L-tone except in the following cases. According to Voorhoeve (1961b, pp.148-153), the exceptions involve underlyingly untoned units occurring between two underlying H-tones in (i) a single non-compound word, and (ii) a compound word, and (iii) a sequence of two syntactically closely related items, e.g. article and noun. In these cases, the untoned units receive H-tone at surface level by means of tone copying. It is interesting to note, in view of the preceding discussion, how non-compound words with more than one underlying H-tone are treated in the same manner as compound words and certain special syntactic structures. It certainly supports the proposition that mono-morphemic words with more than one underlying H-tone developed historically from separate lexical items in combination.

In the operation of the tone-copying rule under discussion, the question arises concerning which one of the two underlying H-tones is involved in the tone-copying rule. In the diagram below which illustrates the operation of the rule, the second H-tone is the one shown as the tone involved in the copying. Justification for this will be presented in the discussion which follows. In (28), the symbol || represents the boundaries around the units within which the tone copying rule applies.

(28)

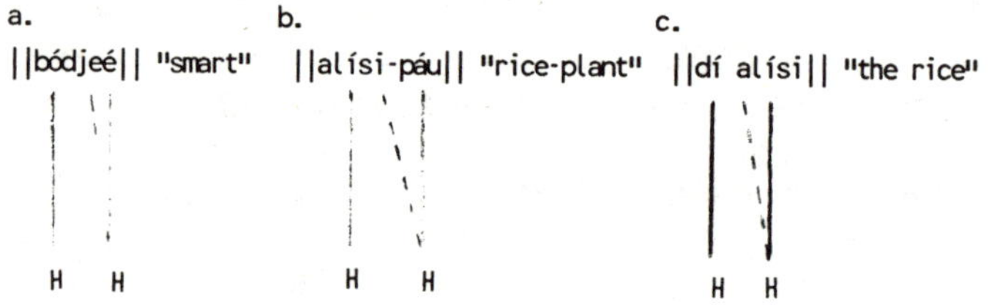

a. ||bódjeé|| "smart"

b. ||alísi-páu|| "rice-plant"

c. ||dí alísi|| "the rice"

    H H   H H   H H

There is, in Saramaccan, a tone reduction rule which applies to underlying H-tones occurring in final position in affirmative sentences. When such H-tones are preceded either by a tone-bearing unit lexically associated with an underlying H, or acquiring H-tone by copying, the sentence final H-tone becomes realised as L at the surface level. (Voorhoeve, 1961b, p.148) In (29), we present words and special syntactic structures in which tone copying operates, and in which there is an underlying H-tone initially associated with the final tone-bearing unit. The first column presents the words and structures in their underlying tonological forms. The second column presents them as they would be realised on the surface sentence internally, and the third column shows the forms they would take in final position in an affirmative sentence.

(29)   Sentence   Sentence
     Underlying   Internal   Final

a. /kúnunú/   [kúnúnú]   [kúnùnù]   "mountain"
b. /bódjeé/   [bódjéé]   [bódjèè]   "smart"
c. /avó-avó/   [àvó-ávó]   [àvó-àvò]   "various ancestors"
d. /mí tatá/   [mí tátá]   [mí tàtà]   "my father"
e. /mí azanganá/ [mí ázángáná] [mí àzàngànà] "my tibia"

(from Voorhoeve, 1961)

H-tone deletion and tone copying are shown in rules (30) and (31) respectively. The units enclosed within ‖ are single or compound words, or a sequence of two syntactically closely related items.

(30) Sentence final H-tone deletion rule

     | X H H | ----> | X H | ——— / $
         1 2   1

(31) Tone copying rule

     | ° | ----> H / | H ——— H |
                   1   2

What is not clear from rule (31), however, is which underlying H-tone is involved in the copying on to the neighbouring zero-specified tone-bearing unit. We could propose that the first of the two underlying H-tones, i.e. H_1 is the one which copies. This proposal would fit in well with the observation of Hyman and Schuh (1974, pp.95-96), that tonal influences, notably copying, tend to be progressive and to move from left to right. However, such a proposal would run into the problem of how to explain the fact that no copying occurs when the second underlying H-tone is deleted in sentence-final position. One would have to propose that the copying rule only applies when underlying H appears on the surface. An alternative proposal would be that it is H_2 which copies leftward. This has the advantage of simplicity since, when the H is deleted, no tone copying can take place, as can be seen from the examples in the third column of (29) above. The disadvantage, however, lies in the fact that this would violate the generalisation that tone copying tends to be progressive in most languages. There is little to choose between the two options, but, for purposes of this work, we shall opt for the former.

Let us now examine the rules governing the assignment of stress in Saramaccan as outlined in (27). According to the first rule, the first heavy syllable within the foot is stressed. As in Djuka, heavy syllables developed in Saramaccan as a result of the deletion of liquids occurring between vowels. The two vowels then merged, creating a single syllable with a long vowel. Evidence presented by Voorhoeve (1961a, p.105), suggests that this process had not yet started in 1805. In (32), we see the early Saramaccan forms alongside their modern equivalents.

(32)	**Early Saramaccan**	**Modern Saramaccan**	
a.	gorón	goón	"ground"
b.	kurúkutu	kuúkutu	"crooked"
c.	tirípa	tiípa	"intestines"

(Voorhoeve, 1961a, p.105)

As pointed out by Smith (1977, p.47) and Alleyne (1980, p.45), the process of intervocalic deletion is far more widespread in Saramaccan than in Djuka. The effect of this would have been to create far more heavy syllables in the former language than in the latter. If we assume that stress was associated with underlying H-tone in Early Saramaccan as it was in

Plantation Creole, the predecessor to Djuka, what would have occurred is clear. The displacement of stress from the syllable containing the vowel associated with the underlying H-tone to the heavy syllable would have occurred far more frequently in Saramaccan than in Djuka. This might suggest a reason as to why, in the absence of a heavy syllable, stress is assigned to the penultimate syllable as stated in (27)b. The frequency with which heavy syllables attracting stress would occur in Saramaccan may have served to nearly completely destroy the link which previously existed between H-tone and stress. One indication that this link did once exist can be seen in stress rule (27)c. This states that, in two-syllable lexical items in which the underlying H-tone is associated with a tone-bearing unit in the second syllable, stress may variably be assigned to the second syllable. The variation involved here is between assigning stress to the penultimate syllable, and to the syllable containing the H-toned vowel. This is the only area in Saramaccan where the link between stress and underlying H-tone has been preserved, albeit in variation.

1.35 Papiamentu

Papiamentu is an Afro-European Creole language spoken in the Netherlands Antilles islands of Aruba, Bonaire and Curacao. The bulk of the vocabulary of this Creole language is of Portuguese/Spanish origin. Portuguese seems to have been the major early source of lexical items in Papiamentu, with Spanish providing the major source for words more recently entering the language. English and Dutch are also sources for some items which have entered the language.

Source material on the question of stress and tone in Papiamentu is rather sketchy. However, Romer (1977), while focusing on tone polarisation in Papiamentu, provides an important source of information on Papiamentu tone presented within a modern framework. From data presented there, it would seem that the vast majority of non-compound lexical items contain a single underlying H-tone. Where such items have an identifiable Spanish / Portuguese cognate, the location of the underlying H-tone in the Papiamentu item corresponds to the position of the stressed syllable in the cognate.

(33)   Papiamentu   Span/Port.
                                              Cognates

    a. /sín/   "without"   'sin
    b. /kás/   "house"   'casa
    c. /léchi/   "milk"   'leche
    d. /nóchi/   "evening"   'noche
    e. /muhé/   "female"   mu'jer
    f. /kansá/   "tired"   can'sado
    g. /buníta/   "beautiful"   bo'nita
    h. /konténtu/   "glad"   con'tento
    i. /konosí/   "well-known"   cono'cer
    j. /karpinté/   "carpenter"   carpin'teiro

Let us now examine briefly the major rules determining the surface forms of zero-specified tone-bearing units in Papiamentu. For such units occurring within a word after the unit lexically associated with the underlying H-tone, two forms are possible. In the environment of a following word beginning with a tone-bearing unit which carries a surface L-tone, the zero specified tone-bearing unit polarizes, being realised with a surface H-tone as in (34)a below. Otherwise, the redundant tone spelling rule applies. This is a rule which appears to operate in Papiamentu redundantly assigning surface L-tone to all zero-specified tone-bearing units (See Romer, 1977, fn.3, p.78).

(34)   a. [sú rùmán mùhé tá bùnítá mùchá]
            /buníta/ ---> [bùnítá]
            "his sister is a beautiful girl"

b. [é kás tà dén káyà grándì]
/káya/ ---> [káyà]
"the house is on Main Street"

Romer (1977, p.78, fn.3) provides three other specific examples of words behaving in the manner illustrated in (34), stating that it is a general process in words which, when in final position in a declarative sentence, end in an H-L sequence. In terms of the analysis being employed in the present work, he is referring to items with an underlying H-tone associated with the penultimate tone-bearing unit followed by a zero-specified word-final tone-bearing unit. Romer's additional examples are presented in (35).

(35) a. /pápa/ "porridge; the Pope"
b. /galíña/ "chicken"
c. /lagadíshi/ "lizard"

The major focus of Romer (1977) is on the polarizing behaviour of grammatical items such as the copula ta, prepositions such as di, ku, na, and pa. The surface tone which is realised on these items is the opposite of the tone of the following tone-bearing unit. Romer (1977, p.75) presents the rule governing the surface tone of these polarizing items (POL) in the following way.

(36) POL ----> [α H] / ___ [α H]

In terms of the analysis presented here, we would treat these polarizing items as zero-specified. As in the case of word-final specified tone-bearing units dealt with in (36) and (37), these polarize in the environment of a following surface L-tone. Otherwise, like the other zero-specified tone-bearing units in Papiamentu, they are redundantly assigned surface L-tone by a low level tone spelling rule. As with the other tonal Afro-European Creole languages examined up to now, there is no need to propose anything more complex than an H vs. zero opposition at the underlying level, with surface tonal forms being predicted by rule. This brings us to the interesting question of the relationship between tone and stress in Papiamentu. Papiamentu seems best described as a language in which stress is associated with H-tone. This is certainly the conclusion which Romer (1977, p.78, fn.) arrives at concerning items with more than one H-toned syllable. He states that, in these cases, there is often an alternating primary-secondary stress pattern on the high-toned syllables. In addition, in relation to words of more than two syllables containing only one underlying H-tone, Romer's data indicates that stress coincides with the location of the H-tone, as in the examples below:

(37)   a.   karpinté   "carpenter"
       b.   Panamá   "Panama"
       c.   teátro   "theatre"
       d.   bentána   "window"
       e.   bináger   "vinegar"

In two-syllable items, if there is a word initial H-tone, stress also becomes associated with the first syllable. As for two-syllable words with final H-tone, however, only some have a stress pattern predictable by the location of the surface H-tone. Below are examples of two-syllable items which follow the expected pattern of H-tone related stress placement, all taken from Romer (1977).

(38)   a.   máta   "plant (noun)"
       b.   pára   "bird"
       c.   pápa   "porridge; the Pope"
       d.   kácho   "dog"
       e.   muhé   "woman"
       f.   piská   "fish (noun)"

There is, however, a special group of two-syllable lexical items with a LH surface tone sequence which does not fit into the general pattern. Significantly, all of these items end in vowels in spite of the fact that Papiamentu does allow word-final closed syllables. In these items, there is vowel lengthening in the first syllable, i.e. the one with the L-tone. Romer (1977, p.78, fn.1) states that in such a low toned syllable, length seems to be the primary phonetic cue for stress. Although not explicitly stated by Romer or anyone else writing on the subject, we will assume that intensity or loudness is the primary phonetic cue for stress in syllables with H-tone. Romer (p. 69) maintains that this special group of items is stressed on the first syllable only. However, Baum (1976, p.87), Goilo (1962, p.11) and Birmingham (1970, p.5) all argue that both syllables in these items receive equal stress, meaning presumably that the intensity with which the two syllables are produced is the same. This view does not really contradict the substance of the Romer position since the latter considers vowel lengthening to be the manifestation of stress on a low-toned syllable, and that the first syllable with H-tone carries primary stress. Within Romer's own framework, therefore, the first syllable can be considered to be stressed by way of vowel lengthening, and the second by means of intensity being associated with the first H-toned syllable in the word. In the examples below of items belonging to this special group of two-syllable items, the first syllable is marked for stress whereas the second can be considered to have stress predicted by the presence of H-tone, and is, therefore, left unmarked.

(39) a. 'també   "too, also"
     b. 'muchá   "boy, girl"
     c. 'numá   "no more, nothing else"
     d. 'amí   "I, me (emphatic)"
     e. 'duná   "(to) give"
     f. 'jamá   "(to) call"
     g. 'sirbí   "(to) serve"
     h. 'puntrá   "(to) ask"

According to Birmingham (1970, p.5), the initial stressed syllable produced with a lengthened vowel has falling pitch. In all this, we are faced with having to propose that, in two syllabe words, both tonal and stress features need to be specified in the lexicon. This is the position taken by Romer (1977, p.69). If this were indeed the correct approach, Papiamentu would join that very select band of tone languages to which West African languages such as Balanta, Dagara and Jarawa belong. This group is made up to tone languages in which unpredictable stress, independent of tone, has been reported. (Meussen 1970, p.268) In fact, however, a much simpler explanation supported by the data presents itself. We may propose that these low-toned syllables contain an underlying H-tone which has been reduced in the environment of an immediately following H-tone. The stress associated with the underlying H-tone is, however, preserved in the form of vowel lengthening by virtue of the fact that the syllable is in the penultimate position within the word. As we have already seen, penultimate position tends to favour the appearance of stress in a wide range of human languages. This analysis is supported by the verbs which belong to this special group of Papiamentu items. It should be noted that apart from a few exceptions, eight listed by Birmingham (1970, p.6), all the items belonging to this category may be described as verbals. When these items function as imperatives, they take H-tone on the initial syllable with a single stress associated with the H-toned syllable.

(40) a. 'matá   "(to) kill"   máta   "Kill!"
      b. 'pará   "(to) stop"   pára   "Stop!"
      c. 'komé   "(to) eat"   kómc   "Eat!"
      d. 'papjá   "(to) speak"   pápja   "Speak!"

In the imperative, we would argue that it is the first H-tone which surfaces, reducing the second. The reason for the absence of stress on the second syllable in these cases lies in the fact that stress associated with a reduced H-tone is only retained in penultimate position. That the behaviour of two-syllable verbs in the imperative is the result of underlying H-tone in the initial/penultimate syllable can be seen from a comparison with the behaviour of three-syllable verbs. In their normal, non-imperative forms, these have a word-final H-tone but no initial or penultimate stress. In the imperative, they do not change their surface tonal form. Thus, kushiná "(to) cook" becomes kushiná "Cook!", with no tonal change in the imperative.

The significance of the penultimate position in the functioning of underlying H-tones which sometimes only surface as stress, can be seen in the fact that all of the members of the special group of two-syllable items end in vowels. Birmingham, (1970, p.8) points out that Papiamentu has a relatively low tolerance for word-final consonants in general, with -r and -s being among the only ones commonly permitted. Even these, however, are often deleted. The tendency towards a preference for open syllables is a common feature in Afro-European Creole languages. (Alleyne, 1980) We can perhaps, therefore, propose that items ending in consonants are underlyingly trisyllabic.

(41)	Underlying		Surface	
a.	injánV	--->	inján	"Indian"
b.	kalórV	--->	kalór	"hot"
c.	kabésV	--->	kabés	"head"
d.	aprélV	--->	aprél	"April"

This could be used to explain why it is that no item ending in a consonant seems to belong to the special group of two-syllable items. In support of this hypothesis, we can examine the behaviour of two-syllable verbs with clitics such as the singular object pronoun forms mi, bo and ɛ. When these verbs appear with these clitics, the verbs do not take the initial syllable stress with which they would otherwise occur. In the case of ɛ, it fuses with the final vowel of the verb creating a two-syllable sequence but the tonal shape of the verb is the same as if three syllables existed on the surface. Below are examples adapted from Bendix (1983, pp.113-116).

(42) a. pa <u>bi</u>sámi eséi   "to tell me that"
     b. ta 'amí a-<u>du</u>nábo ɛ   "It is I who gave you it"
     c. nos un <u>mi</u>rɛ́ ('mirá + ɛ) "We didn't see it"

From the examples in (40) and (42), an important generalisation can be made. The initial underlying H-tone in these special two-syllable items can only surface in environments where initial stress is possible. This is supported by evidence from imperative forms of two-syllable verbs which take clitics such as the singular personal pronoun object. In these cases, there is no initial-syllable H-tone appearing on the surface, even though it does appear in imperative forms which do not take these clitics.

(43) a. lagámi só   "Leave me alone!"
     b. jamámi   "Call me!"
     c. komé ('komɛ + ɛ)   "Eat it!"

Tone seems to be playing a subordinate role to stress in these instances. This is the opposite of the kind of relationship that one would expect in a tone language, or the one that exists between tone and stress in the other areas of Papiamentu. The relationship between stress and tone in these two-syllable verbs has a lot more in common with the link which exists between stress and high pitch in stress accent languages. In these languages, high pitch is just one of the ways in which stress may be manifested at the surface level. In spite of all this, however, it is probably more economical to analyse the behaviour of these special two-syllable items in tonal terms in a language which, apart from this special group of items, is entirely tonal. The analysis would have to be that initial H-tone in these two-syllable items (i) is realised on the surface in certain environments, e.g. imperatives without clitics, (ii) is reduced leaving H-tone associated stress behind, e.g. in the non-imperative forms of the verbs without clitics, and (iii) is deleted where a third syllable, usually in the form of a clitic, is attached to the verb. The rules governing the assignment of stress in Papiamentu would, therefore, be as follows.

(44) Papiamentu stress assignment rule

> Assign stress to every surface H-toned syllable, to every syllable with a reduced underlying H-tone, but not to those with H-tones which have been deleted.

In spite of the above, it has to be admitted that Papiamentu has had its tonal system influenced by the introduction of stress independent of H-tone. The question is, of course, whether this occurred in the original contact situation which gave rise to the development of Papiamentu as a language, or as a result of modern day contact with Spanish. If we explore the first possibility to begin with, we find, as is noted by Taylor (1977, pp.176-177) and Traill and Ferraz (1981, p.208, fn.1), some verbs in Afro-Iberian Creole languages are derived from Iberian infinitive forms and others from the third person singular indicative. In the Iberian languages, infinitives take final stress and the third person forms stress on the penultimate syllable. It could be argued, therefore, that in the initial contact between speakers of West African tone languages and speakers of Portuguese, the former interpreted the two positions in which stress could occur in verb forms as indicating the presence of penultimate stress followed by underlying H-tone. When, in certain structures such as the imperative, the underlying H-tone was deleted, penultimate stress became realised on the surface as H-tone.

The evidence from Papiamentu, however, seems to favour the alternative explanation. In the examples below in (45) taken from Birmingham (1970), we have minimal pairs involving two-syllable verb-type items, one with initial stress and the other without.

(45)   a. ɛ ta 'sintá   "He (she) is sitting"
           ɛ ta sintá   "He (she) is seated"

       b. ɛ ta 'hasí trabów "He (she) is doing work"
           trabów ta hasí   "The work is done"

       c. mi ta 'skirbí   "I am writing"
           búki ta skirbí   "The book is written"

This kind of distinction between a verb and what may be described as a past participle is extremely unusual for Afro-European Creoles. This suggests decreolisation in Papiamentu involving influence from Iberian -ido and -ado past participle endings.

One could suggest underlying forms for the items above without initial stress such as *sintado, *hasido, and *skirbido. Such forms would make the initial syllable not penultimate at the underlying level, and would explain the absence of word-initial stress in the past participle forms. What justification, however, is there from within the language for proposing such underlying forms? According to Birmingham (1970, p.94), in Papiamentu items etymologically derived from Iberian -er conjugation verbs, there is generally the etymological i in the past participle forms, but not in the ordinary verb form. The examples in (46) demonstrate this.

(46)   a. 'komɛ́   "(to) eat"   komí   "eaten"
        b. 'sabɛ́   "(to) know"   sabí   "known"
        c. konosɛ́ "(to) know"   konosí "known"
        d. optené "(to) get"   optení "obtained"

Birmingham uses data such as this to argue that Papiamentu past participle forms contain -ado and -ido endings which have been subject to apocope. The notion of two-syllable past participle type forms such as sintá "seated" and komɛ́ "eaten" being underlyingly trisyllabic would certainly serve to explain why they take no word-initial stress. Influence from

Portuguese after the development of Papiamentu as a language, or more recent influence from Spanish with which Papiamentu is presently in contact, may serve to explain the source of this distinction between verb and past participle forms.

The question would arise, in all this, of why three-syllable verbs do not have a penultimate stressed syllable followed by H-tone, since penultimate stress in the third person singular operates for verbs of any number of syllables in the Iberian languages. The answer has to be that, for the pre- H-tone stress to occur, the syllable to which it would attach itself must not only be penultimate but initial. Hyman (1975, p.209) points out that the two positions to which stress is most normally attracted in human languages are the initial and penultimate slots. For lexically contrastive stress to appear in what is otherwise a tone language with predictable stress, the innovation had to occur where there was a coincidence of these two most favoured environments.

Even though this special group of two-syllable items is largely made up of verbs, there is a small number of non-verbals which behave in a similar manner. Examples have been presented in (39) a-d. An explanation of the origin of the behaviour of these non-verbals may be that, with the developing of the 'H sequence among verbs, a new stress/tone pattern was now available within the language. This pattern may be in the process of spreading to certain non-verbal items.

What exists in Papiamentu, outside the special group of two-syllable items, is a system involving an opposition between syllables specified with an underlying H-tone and those with zero-specification. Generally, lexical items in Papiamentu have only one syllable associated with an underlying H-tone. Where these items have cognates in European languages with stress accent, the syllable with underlying H-tone tends to coincide with the stressed syllable in the European language. Papiamentu items appearing to contain more than one underlying H-tone are usually better described as compounds. The surface level realization of zero-specified syllables is determined by low level phonological rules. In relation to the assignment of stress, H-toned syllables are redundantly marked for stress. This is the case in all areas of the language except for the special category of two-syllable items where stress on a zero-specified syllable needs to be marked within the lexicon.

1.4. A Synthesis And Some Conclusions

The theory originally put forward was that when a language variety arises out of contact between a stress accent language and a tonal language or languages, and in which the bulk of the vocabulary of the new language is borrowed from the stress accent language, a tone language with incomplete tonification is what is likely to emerge. These new languages would need entries in the lexicon which would specify the location of, at most, one underlying H-tone, corresponding to the location of stress accent in words originating in the stress language. The tonal shape of the zero-specified syllables is assigned by low level tone spelling rules. This kind of language is what, in many traditional approaches, may have been termed a tonal accent language.

The question is, of course, how well did the Afro-English and Afro-Portuguese/Spanish Creole languages examined fit into the model? In addition, what modifications do we need to make to the original theoretical model in the light of the facts of these languages. Sranan, of course, stands out from all the others as being the sole language variety discussed which has been described as having a stress accent system. The fact that Djuka, another English-lexicon Creole language spoken in Surinam, is tonal is quite significant. Djuka is both historically related to Sranan and, at present, still very similar to it. The other, more distantly related Creole language of Surinam, Saramaccan, is also tonal. When one adds to this the fact that tonal analyses have been proposed for a range of Afro-English Creole languages spoken across the Caribbean and in West Africa, all showing a greater degree of modern day influence from English than does Sranan, the presence of a stress accent system in Sranan seems rather surprising. If the analyses of this language as involving stress accent are indeed accurate, this must have developed out of a system which was originally tonal.

Principense represents quite clearly a system of prominence based on the vowel rather than the syllable. The distinction is significant since this language has long vowels, either portion of which can be lexically marked for prominence by means of high pitch. In Principense, the location of prominence in words with Portuguese cognates usually corresponds to the position of stress accent in the Portuguese equivalents. Because, however, the unit of prominence in Principense is the vowel rather than the syllable, one is dealing with a system of tonal prominence rather than one involving stress. The Principense system as described by Traill and Ferraz (1981) seems to be an entirely accentual one, differing from stress accent only in the unit being marked for prominence. There is, therefore, no justification for proposing the existence of an underlying H-tone. This language is thus a true tonal accent one like, for example, Somali (Hyman 1981), rather than one involving any degree of incomplete tonification. This shift from a system such as that operating in Principense to the one operating in Sranan simply involves the loss of long vowels, a process which has been demonstrated to have occurred in the latter language and to be occurring in Principense.

But by what means does a language with incomplete tonification involving the existence of a single underlying H-tone per word become a tonal accent language with no underlying H-tone? In order to discover this process let us use languages such as Djuka as the point of departure. We have already established that the introduction of heavy syllables by way of development of long vowels occurred relatively early in the history of this language. Prior to this introduction, the presence of underlying H-tone would automatically have attracted stress. After, however, heavy syllables took precedence in the assignment of stress, with stress only being associated with underlying H-tone in the absence of a heavy syllable. (See 1.33) As has been pointed out in the discussion connected with the examples in (23), Djuka H-tone appears to have been attracted to the first vowel of any heavy syllable occurring to its right. Nevertheless, stress and the location of underlying H-tone in Djuka did remain partly independent of each other as in <u>toosí</u> "push", with stress being associated with the heavy syllable rather than the one with H-tone.

Let us examine what would happen if a language such as Djuka began to lose its heavy syllables made up of long vowels, as a result of decreolisation. Logically, the first such syllables which are likely to disappear are those which do not contain an underlying H-tone. The presence of an underlying H-tone in a long vowel would tend to attract stress and to favour, as a result, the retention of the heavy syllable. What would have developed is a language made up of light syllables, on the one hand, and heavy syllables containing a double vowel sequence, on the other. However, the latter syllable type would only occur with H-tone. H-tone would, however, be able to occur in both light and heavy syllables. With the disappearance of non-H-toned heavy syllables, H-tone and stress would always occur in the same syllable.

Even if those who were already speakers of the language while this change was taking place may have continued to view stress as predictable in relation to the location of the H-tone, this is not the generalisation which a new generation of speakers of the language would have made. They would notice that heavy syllables provide a natural phonological environment for the occurrence of stress, and would conclude that it is the presence of stress on such syllables which predicts H-tone. They would extend this analysis to light syllables with H-tone, concluding that it is the stress on these syllables which predicts H-tone. The only reason for continuing to regard such a system as tonal is the fact that the unit of prominence continues to be the vowel rather than the syllable. In other words, either vowel in a heavy syllable can be marked for prominence by means of high pitch. This, however, is no longer a language with incomplete tonification involving an H vs. zero opposition. Rather, it is a tonal accent language, the vowel rather than the syllable being marked for prominence as would be the case in a stress accent system. Principense is precisely such a language.

What is being proposed here is that, in Surinam, for example, there was a historical development which involved Plantation Creole, a language with incomplete tonification like modern Djuka and Saramaccan, developing heavy syllables involving double vowels by way of intervocalic consonant deletion. With the loss of heavy syllables not containing an underlying H-tone, a tonal accent language much like Principense is what would have developed as a precursor to modern Sranan. As a result of further syllabic restructuring, as is presently taking place in Principense as a result of Portuguese influence (Traill and Ferraz 1981, pp.213-214, fn.10), one of the vowels in two vowel sequences becomes replaced by a liquid. The effect would have been the disappearance of the syllable with the long vowel, and the creation of a system of marking prominence whose domain is the syllable rather than the vowel. The stress accent system of a language like Sranan would be the natural outcome of such a process.

The development of heavy syllables by way of the weakening and deletion of intervocalic consonants or as a result of compensatory lengthening, seems quite restricted in Afro-European Creole languages. It has not been reported in any of the other Afro-English varieties spoken in the Caribbean or in varieties such as Krio in West Africa. The Surinam varieties, Djuka and Saramaccan, seem quite isolated in this regard. Such syllables do not seem to have developed in Papiamentu either, in spite of their presence in Principense, a related Afro-Portuguese language. This may explain why Papiamentu, in spite of influence from Spanish at the level of syllable structure and stress placement, has remained essentially a language with incomplete tonification involving an opposition between underlying H-tone and zero specification. It is suggested in 1.35 that the way in which Papiamentu may have accommodated to external language influence is by introducing a special category of two-syllable word with a 'H sequence in which the placement of initial stress needs to be lexically specified.

French is a language with fixed stress. The major acoustic cue for stress in this language is length, though high pitch may sometimes be involved. Stress in French always falls on the last syllable of the word or the sense group. (Rigault, 1970, pp.2-3; Boudreault, 1970, pp.22-25) One would expect, therefore, within the terms of the approach being proposed here, that Afro-European Creole languages with a predominantly French vocabulary base would not require lexical specification for the location of H-tone. If French stress were re-interpreted by speakers of West African tone languages as H-tone, such H-tones would invariably occur in word or phrase final position. In fact, as far as can be ascertained, no French lexicon Afro-European Creole language has been described as employing any lexically significant means of marking prominence, whether in the form of tone or stress. Where prosodic features have even been discussed in phonological descriptions of these languages, the role of tone or stress operating in a manner which is lexically significant has been explicitly dismissed. (Valdman, 1978, p.52) St. Lucian French lexicon Creole has been described as having predictable stress at the end of a word or phrase (Carrington, 1984, p.44), and Haitian has been treated as being able to receive accentuation on any syllable within the word or phrase depending on the requirements of intonation. (Ariza, 1980)

What all this establishes is that, in the area of the development of tonal systems in Afro-European Creole languages, it took two to tango. The fact that tonal systems were an essential feature of the native languages of the West Africans involved in the early contact situation, did not guarantee that the Creole language which developed would also employ tone in a lexically significant manner. Only when the European language which provided the bulk of the vocabulary for the contact language itself had lexically significant stress, could native speakers of tone languages re-interpret this as H-tone. It is, of course, only when this re-interpretation is made that a Creole language requiring that the location of underlying H-tone be lexically specified could emerge.

Chapter 2

A Tonal Analysis Of Guyanese Creole

2.0 Introduction

Guyanese Creole (GC) is an Afro-European Creole language which developed as a result of contact between Niger-Congo languages on one hand, and English on the other. As has been pointed out in Chap. 1, tone is an integral part of the phonological systems of the more conservative Afro-English Creole languages such as Saramaccan and Djuka. GC has been subject to some amount of decreolisation as a result of pressure from English, the official high-prestige languages alongside which it exists in Guyana. The question, therefore, arises as to whether a tonal as opposed to a stress accent system has managed to survive in GC. In the event that a tonal system has survived, what kind of effect has continued influence from English had on this system?

In order to effectively answer these questions, this chapter first attempts to trace the evolution of the GC syllable structure up to the present. This is necessary since it is the syllable or constituents of the syllable which would be bearers of either stress or tonal features. It is against this background that we address the issue of tone in GC. The chapter attempts to deal with the historical processes by which tone has acquired its present status in GC and proposes a descriptive model which would account for tonal behaviour within the language.

2.1 The Syllable And The Mora

Alleyne (1980, p.76) presents a reconstruction of the basic vowel system of proto-varieties of Afro-English Creole languages. The reconstruction resembles and is based on the vowel system of modern Saramaccan, the most conservative of the modern Afro-English Creole language varieties.

(47) **Proto Afro-English Creole Vowel System**

```
      i              u
       e          o
        ɛ       ɔ
           a
```

It is observed by Alleyne (1980, pp.39-41) that the lower mid vowels in Saramaccan occur mainly in words of African origin. He concludes that this would also have been the case in the earliest Afro-English varieties. The number of words of African origin in Djuka is much reduced when compared with Saramaccan. In Djuka, therefore, the functional load carried by the phonemic distinction between upper-mid and lower-mid vowels would have been considerably less than that of any earlier stage similar to Saramaccan. This would have created the conditions for the disappearance of the height distinction among mid vowels. Djuka, in fact, has a system of five vowel phonemes with only one set of mid vowels. Varieties such as GC with even fewer items of African origin than Djuka would, therefore, have developed a Djuka-type vowel system at some point in their history. Such a system, as it would have emerged in proto-GC, is presented in (48) below.

(48) **Proto-GC Vowel System**

```
      i              u
       e          o
           a
```

Saramaccan and Djuka have complex syllabic nuclei made up of two vowels. However, as has been mentioned in Chap. 1, these are a relatively new development in these languages, coming about as a result of the deletion of certain intervocalic consonants. Before this, the sole form of the nucleus in these two conservative Afro-English Creoles involved a single vowel. What this suggests is that the earlier Afro-English varieties such as Proto-GC also employed a single vowel as the only possible syllabic nucleus. This is presented in (49).

(49) **The Proto-GC Nucleus**

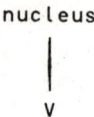

Two particular features of the phonological system of a decreolised variety of Afro-English Creole such as GC should be noted. The first is that it possesses a larger number of vowels than earlier more conservative varieties. Secondly, it allows for complex syllabic nuclei. The introduction of these two features into the language under the continued influence of English, has been noted in the literature, e.g. Alleyne (1980). What has not occurred, however, is that these two developments be seen not as a pair of distinct phenomena, but as part of the same process. It is the link between the two that we will now seek to establish and explore.

Let us first examine the phonetic forms of the vowel phonemes in GC. These are presented in (50).

(50) **GC Vowel Phonemes (Phonetically represented)**

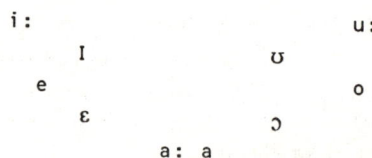

In the pairs of vowels [i:] and [I], [u:] and [ʊ], [e:] and [ɛ], as well as [o:] and [ɔ], the second member in each case is lower, more centralised and shorter. The features of relative height, proximity to the periphery of the mouth i.e. tenseness, as well as length, coincide in GC as they do in many languages. The question which arises is that of which one of these features is primary in GC. The pair [a:] and [a], differing as they do only in length, establishes that length is, in fact, the primary feature. In non-low pairs, the longer vowel will be slightly higher and produced closer to the periphery of the mouth. We now have a basis for normalising the presentation of the vowel system of GC with length rather than height or degree of centralisation as the feature distinguishing these pairs. This normalised GC vowel chart is presented below.

(51) **GC Vowel Phonemes (normalised)**

```
ii    i              u    uu
  ee    e          o   oo
           a:    a
```

This presentation of the GC vowel phonemes suggests a strong similarity with the proto-GC type vowel system presented in (48). Such a similarity is clearly not surprising. The difference between the two systems is that GC has developed a vowel length contrast which did not exist at the proto-GC stage. Interestingly enough, there is another change which has taken place in the syllable structure of GC. Modern GC allows for consonants in post-vocalic position. This has come about by way of final vowel deletion produced by influence from English cognates which are consonant final. Thus, proto-GC */futu/ > GC /fut/ "foot", proto-GC */bigi/ > GC /big/ "big", proto-GC */goni/ > GC /gon/ "gun", etc. By way of support for these reconstructions, it should be pointed out that these proto-GC forms also occur in modern Djuka.

The fact that modern GC permits syllables to contain long vowels, diphthongs and vowel followed by consonant, suggests that one major change has taken place relative to proto-Djuka. Branching nuclei have been introduced into the language, the second member of the nucleus being either a vowel or a consonant.

It is important, at this point, to say a few words about the theoretical approach within which this analysis is taking place. Clements & Keyser (1983, p.8, p.136) argue for the idea that syllables can be viewed from the perspective of what they refer to as a CV-tier. The V-elements on such a tier dominate segments which function as syllable peaks. The C-elements dominate segments which function as non-peaks, i.e. segments on the margin of the syllable. Unless otherwise stipulated by the grammar or lexicon of a particular language, V-elements are freely allowed to dominate [-consonantal] segments. C-elements, on the other hand, can freely dominate both [+consonantal] segments and [+high, -consonantal] segments, i.e. semi-vowels. (Clements & Keyser, 1983, p.32)

Within the approach just outlined, the nucleus is a prosodic category within the syllable made up of the sequence V(X), with X either representing a single V or C. The choice of V or C as the second element in the nucleus depends on language specific rules. In English, the second element in the nucleus is a C. Justification for this can be found in syllable-final sequences involving three consonants following a short vowel. The final consonant in these clusters must be [+coronal]. Thus, /nekst/ "next" and /glimps/ "glimpse" are well-formed, whereas words like */neksp/ and */glimpf/ are not. In the case of syllable final clusters of two consonants following a long vowel or diphthong, the final consonant is subject to the same constraint, i.e. that it must be [+coronal]. Thus, there is /paynt/ "pint" and /fiynd/ "fiend" but not */paynk/ or */fiymp/. It is clear that the second element in a nucleus containing a long vowel or a diphthong is functioning as a consonant. That second element in the nucleus is, therefore, a C in English rather than a V. (Clements & Keyser, 1983, p.12, pp.33-34)

In GC, syllable-final consonant clusters which do not include a liquid cannot consist of more than two consonants. The first member must be [-continuant], [-strident], i.e. nasal and oral stops. Two options are available in relation to the second consonant. One option is that it can possess the same coronal and anterior features as the first, but take the opposite voicing, e.g. /kyamp/ "camp", /strims/ "shrimp", /hont/ "hunt", /ans/ "ant(s)", /taŋk/ "tank", /kuŋs/ "faeces". The other option is for it to agree in voicing with the previous consonant but be [+coronal], [+anterior] and have the opposite continuant and strident values to the preceding consonant, e.g. /momz/ "a form of address", /fabz/ "fob", /krips/ "crisp, good", /bonz/ "bun", /gudz/ "goods", /gots/ "guts", /doŋz/ "a type of fruit", /hoks/ "husk", /ragz/ "rags".

In GC, unlike in English, the behaviour of syllable final clusters as outlined above is in no way affected by the kind of vowel nucleus which precedes. They can all occur after branching nuclei, be these long vowels or diphthongs. Thus, the forms /paans/ "trousers", /geens/ "against", /puuŋs/ "a silly person", /plaant/ "plant" and /naint/ "anoint" occur in the language. Other examples include /puups/ "a fool", /jeemz/ "James", /stoonz/ "testicles", /aaks/ "ask", and /lainz/ "contacts".

From the above, it is clear that the second element in a complex nucleus in GC does not function as a consonant. The same consonant clusters can occur after such an element as can occur after the first element in a nucleus. One can only conclude that, in contrast to English, this second element in a complex nucleus is a V. Within the approach being adopted here, we will have to propose, based on the evidence examined, that there is a language specific rule operating in GC which allows a V-element to dominate a [+consonantal] segment. (Clements & Keyser, 1983, p.32)

All this does not only have implications for the

second V-element within a GC nucleus. It also affects what can occur as the first V-element in a nucleus. Modern GC allows all consonantal sonorants with the exception of /r/ to be dominated by the first V-element in a nucleus. As a result, one has items such as /oopm̩/ "open", /sodn̩/ "sudden", /kŋ̩/ "a small quantity", and /bitl̩/ "food". In these examples, all the consonantal sonorants, /m̩/,/n̩/, /ŋ̩/ and /l̩/, function as syllable peaks in non-branching nuclei. The V-element in a simple or non-branching nucleus such as shown below can, therefore, dominate either a vowel or a consonantal sonorant.

(52) **Simple Nuclei In GC**

```
    nuc
     |
     V
```

It has already been established that, in GC, the second element in a complex nucleus is a V, and can dominate either vowel or consonant segments. We can, therefore, represent the complex nuclei in GC in the following way.

(53) **Complex Nuclei In GC**

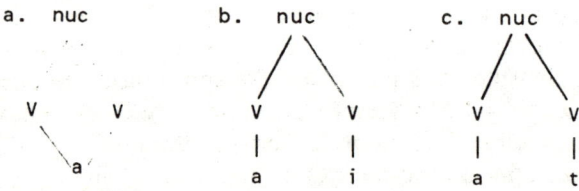

In (53a), /a/ is dominated by both V-elements within the nucleus, indicating that what is produced is the long vowel /aa/. This kind of analysis would also apply to the other long vowels /ii/, /ee/, /oo/ and /uu/. As for (53b), each of the V-elements in the nucleus dominates a different vowel, accounting for the two dipthongs in the language, /ai/ and

/ou/.

In (53c) what is presented is a nucleus with the first V-element dominating a vowel, and the second dominating /t/, which represents any consonant which could occur in post-vocalic position within the syllable. The diagram would account for complex nuclei in items such as /stad/ "showy male", /spit/ "spit", /bed/ "bed", /bon/ "burn", /pul/ "pull", etc.

At this stage, we can state that the continued influence of English on proto-GC seems to have triggered a single phonological change, the introduction of branching nuclei. The second element in such nuclei, we have argued, is a V. It has been established that this applies to nuclei made up of long vowels, with one vowel being dominated by both V-elements. In the case of diphthongs, one vowel functions as the first V-element and a different one as the second. The proposal that a second V-element rather than a C-element was introduced into proto-GC to form complex nuclei makes sense from the point of view of the way in which languages change. A language with a nucleus made up of a single V is more likely to develop a complex nucleus in the way that has occurred in GC. The element which was already a constituent of the nucleus was repeated instead of an entirely new constituent being introduced. The cases of Djuka and Saramaccan in Chap. 1 provide important parallels.

Clements & Keyser (1983, p.80) define the mora as any element on the CV-tier dominated by the node "Nucleus". In other words, each element in the nucleus could be said to constitute a mora. In a simple nucleus containing just a V-element, only one mora exists. In a complex nucleus, on the other hand, in which there is a second element, be it a V as in GC or a C as in English, two moras exist.

There is a problem with this approach, however. How does one deal with the difference between light syllables, i.e. syllables containing a non-branching nucleus, and heavy syllables, i.e. those with a branching nucleus? The distinction could be that languages which are sensitive to syllable weight treat syllables with one mora differently from those with two. It is stated by de Chene (1985, pp.70-73), that there is no principled way of distinguishing between rules of accentuation which are sensitive to the mora and those which respond to syllable weight. Clements & Keyser (1983, p.32) seem uncomfortable with this proposition. They suggest that some languages allow post-vocalic consonants to be dominated by V if such consonants belong to the same syllable as the preceding vowel. They argue that languages of this type are those in which the mora is a unit of prosodic organisation capable of bearing pitch or tone contrasts. Lithuanian, Japanese and Akan are the languages they identify as being of this type.

All this points to the following conclusion which is, however, not explicitly stated by Clements & Keyser (1983). Languages which are sensitive to the mora as opposed to syllable weight have V as the second element in a complex nucleus. Syllable-weight languages would be those with a C as the second element in a complex nucleus. Based on the earlier observation that the V-element represents the category "syllable peak", a nucleus with a VV structure would have two peaks. This would mean that pitch and tone features could be assigned to each V-element separately. Since the C-element represents the functional category "syllable margin", any nucleus of the type 'VC' will have only one peak. Pitch, tone or accentual phenomena could have only one possible point of association in such a nucleus, i.e. with the single possible V-element.

There are two possible ways in which a language can employ the mora as an element in its prosodic system. In the first case, as in languages like Saramaccan and Djuka, it could allow both V-elements in a complex nucleus to potentially be treated in the same way. Thus, in these two languages, underlying H-tone, subject to lexical specification, can appear on either V within a complex nucleus. Association with the first mora in Saramaccan produces a falling surface tone over a syllable with a complex nucleus. In Djuka, this association produces a surface high tone over the entire syllable. In the event of the underlying H-tone being associated with the second mora, a rising tone is produced over the entire syllable in both these languages.

The second possibility is that only a particular mora in a syllable with a complex nucleus can receive tonal specification within a language. The other mora, by contrast, does not receive it. Japanese is such a language. In an accented syllable containing two moras, i.e. a VV nucleus, it is the first which phonetically always receives high pitch, and the second low. (McCawley, 1978, p.114) Even though it is the syllable which receives tonal accent in Japanese, where there are two V-elements within the same syllable, two syllable peaks exist. It is necessary, therefore, that phonetically they receive different treatment. The same is true, as we shall see in the next section, for a language like GC.

By contrast, let us examine what happens in a language like English. Its complex nuclei are made up of VC sequences. Accentual phenomena in such a syllable would have only one V-element with which it can associate. This means that phonetically an accented syllable with a branching nucleus would have exactly the same realisation as one with a simple nucleus. It is for this reason that English is a stress rather than a tonal accent language. As Lass (1984, p.261) points out, the domain of stress is the syllable.

In de Chene (1985, p.56), it is argued that sensitivity to the mora as distinct from the syllable, comes about historically as a result of syllable conflation rules of the form CVCV > CV: and CVCV > CVC. In the first of these rules, a single syllable with a complex nucleus is created by the deletion of an inter-vocalic consonant. In the second, vowel syncope produces a single syllable with a complex nucleus out of what was previously two syllables. GC does not quite fit this model.

The second of the two rules, involving vowel syncope did, as we have already seen, apply historically in the development of GC. However, long vowels did not develop as a result of inter-vocalic consonant reduction. Rather, they entered the language as a result of pressure from English, the language with which GC has coexisted for almost two centuries.

2.2 The Impact Of Syllabic Restructuring On The Tonal System

The question which arises from our discussion of syllabic restructuring is the impact which this has had on the tonal system of GC. In order to deal with this, we need to do some reconstruction of the stress system of proto-GC. Ideally, such a system should share much in common with the stress system of modern Djuka. The problem is, however, that the information available on stress in Djuka (Huttar & Huttar, 1972) is incomplete. Nevertheless, the reconstruction which follows can be reconciled with what is known of Djuka stress.

Every syllable with an underlying H-tone would have received stress in proto-GC. In modern Djuka, only in the environment of a syllable with a complex nucleus within the same word does an underlyingly H-toned syllable not receive stress. Of course, no such environment would have existed in proto-GC since it did not possess syllables with complex nuclei.

Every word made up of more one syllable in proto-GC would have been required to be marked by stress. Where such words contained an underlying H-tone, the location of stress could be predicted. However, it is likely that there were items of more than one syllable which did not possess an underlyingly H-toned syllable. Such items would have received stress on the penultimate syllable. Penultimate stress would have been employed, in the absence of H-tone related stress, as a means of establishing the existence of the item as a separate word. The word boundary at the end of the word is marked by penultimate stress.

Such words, though non-existent in modern GC, do occur albeit rather rarely within Djuka. The examples in Djuka provided by Huttar & Huttar (1972, p.7) are /buku/ "type of mushroom" and /sabaku/ "wading bird". Both appear to be of non-European origin. When one considers the much more extensive loss of non-European vocabulary in GC, it is not surprising that such items no longer exist.

It is clear from the above that the conditions for applying the penultimate stress rule would have been restricted in proto-GC to the small class of word without an underlying H-tone. However, the requirement to signal word boundaries would have existed elsewhere. In words with more than one syllable following an underlying H-tone, the boundary at the end of the word would have been marked by the fact that it was here that the copying of the underlying H-tone came to an end. Stress may, however, have been used to mark the word-initial boundary in words with two or more syllables preceding the underlying H-tone.

There is reason for proposing that the number of preceding syllables should be more than one. Word-initial stress on a syllable immediately preceding one stressed as a result of the presence of an underlying H-tone, would have been subject to stress reduction. Languages usually tend to avoid stress on adjacent syllables.

Hyman (1975, p.208) states that initial and penultimate positions are the most natural phonological environments for demarcative stress. The initial position would, of course, be the most natural position for marking off word-initial boundaries. What all this means is that any word in proto-GC of three syllables or more could have been marked by up to two stresses. The first would have been on the word-initial syllable. The second would have been on that syllable associated with underlying H-tone when it occurred in third position or later. In order to explain some of the tonal facts of modern GC, this is the proposal being made here.

The fact that every syllable contained a nucleus made up of a single V-element means that either the vowel or the syllable could be regarded as the tone-bearing unit. On the other hand, the domain of stress is always the syllable, and this would, therefore, have been true for stress in proto-GC.

In addition to loudness and length as acoustic cues for stress, we can, based on our knowledge of modern GC, identify an additional stress cue. A syllable following one which was stressed would have been slightly lower in pitch than if it had followed an unstressed syllable. The employment of pitch differences to signal stress is not unusual in tone languages. For example, Carter (1983, p.101) refers to Tonga which signals stress on an H-toned syllable by raising the pitch with which it is produced.

With the introduction of syllabic nuclei with the structure VV into GC, the phonetic feature of lowered pitch on that which followed continued to be associated with the V-element which had always received it, i.e. the first V. The result of this is that in modern GC a fall in pitch from the first V to the second V is a marker of stress in syllables with VV nuclei In a syllable with a simple nucleus, i.e. a nucleus possessing a single V-element, a pitch fall occurs on the following syllable, if any. The introduction of VV nuclei has made pitch lowering a feature of the mora or V rather than the syllable.

Word initial stress, in the circumstances just described, would have as one of its manifestations pitch lowering. The first mora of the stressed syllable would cause the following mora to have lowered pitch. How could this now be distinguished from the rule assigning underlying H-tone? The latter would also be assigned to the first mora of the nucleus. What is being suggested here is that word initial stress had become converted into the marking of prominence on the first mora of the first syllable. As Hyman (1981, p.200) points out, however, assigning prominence to the mora rather than the syllable is a tonal rather than a stress phenomenon. Thus, in a word with an underlying H-tone two or more syllables from the beginning, word initial stress became reinterpreted as tonal and treated as an underlying H-tone which had become reduced in the presence of a following one. From being a language which allowed a maximum of one underlying H-tone per word, GC had become reinterpreted as allowing for up to two such tones. Where both occurred, the first was reduced, i.e. did not receive a surface H-tone. However, the first mora of such a syllable would be produced with higher pitch than would the following moras bearing the same surface tone.

What is being proposed here is the reinterpretation of word-initial stress as underlying H-tone (UHT) in a system which is already tonal. This process is quite a plausible one as we would see if we look at the historical development of languages such as Japanese and Classical Greek. Old Japanese, as late as the 10th century, was a language without closed syllables or a vowel length contrast. (de Chene, 1985, p.73) Sound changes subsequently took place, introducing long vowels and closed syllables. This resulted in the system of assigning tonal accent in modern Japanese. The first mora of the accented syllable is H-toned. The following moras within the word receive Low tone. This is regardless of whether the accented syllable has two moras or not. In syllables with the complex VV nuclei allowed by modern Japanese, the first vowel, the portion of the nucleus which had been part of the accented syllable in Old Japanese, continues to be accented. The restructuring of the Japanese syllabic nucleus had produced a mora-based accentual system out of one which had been syllable-based.

Hyman (1981, p.200) argues against the proposals of Oomen (1981) concerning the origin of tonal accent in Somali. He agonises over the problem of how tonal accent could be introduced into a language, speculating that it may have been developed as a result of the loss of a laryngeal or pharyngeal segment in word-final position. He, however, admits that he has no concrete evidence for this. Somali, is a language with long vowels and diphthongs. Hyman (1981, pp.171-172 fn.) presents evidence that inter-vocalic semi-vowel deletion had taken place in the language, producing syllabic nuclei made up of two vowels. This process may have previously applied to a much wider range of inter-vocalic consonants in the language. As with Japanese, it could be argued that stress accent associated with the syllable became associated with that portion of the VV nucleus into which the syllable had been absorbed. The new domain of accent had thus become the vowel rather than the syllable, and a tonal accent system had emerged out of a stress accent one.

The reinterpretation of word initial stress as UHT as a result of syllabic restructuring, triggered far-reaching changes in the tonal system of GC. Proto-GC had been a language which allowed a maximum of one UHT per lexical item. Modern GC, however, allows up to two UHTs per lexical item. The restrictions on the occurrences of UHTs in the modern language are all closely related to the way in which the new tonal system had emerged. The rule for assigning the first UHT to an item within the lexicon can be expressed in the following way.

(54) Initial underlying H-tone assignment rule

> Optionally assign initial UHT to the first syllable of the item, depending on lexical specification. If not assigned to the first syllable, assign obligatorily to the second syllable, if any.

What does this signify? The initial UHT in GC has to be assigned to either the first or the second syllable. This is directly traceable back to the way in which the new GC tonal system emerged. Demarcative stress on the first syllable had become converted to UHT. At the same time, when a UHT occurred on the second syllable of the item, word-initial demarcative stress became reduced in the environment of the adjacent syllable with UHT. This syllable would itself have received stress as a result of the UHT. With the introduction of an initial UHT into the language, the first two syllables of the word became its domain.

The initial UHT assignment rule in (54) allows for the following two possibilities for items with more than one syllable, (i) initial UHT on the first syllable and (ii) initial UHT on the second syllable. How does one, however, fit the behaviour of monosyllables into all this? A monosyllable in GC may or may not have a UHT, depending on lexical specification. It has already been noted that the domain of the initial UHT is the first two syllables. A monosyllabic item with UHT would, therefore, be regarded by speakers in the same way as an item of two syllables with initial UHT on the first syllable. A monosyllable without UHT would, on the other hand, be regarded in the same way as the first syllable of a two syllable sequence with UHT on the second syllable. We will be better able to understand this after considering the assignment rule for non-initial UHT.

(55) Non-initial underlying H-tone assignment rule

Optionally assign, depending on lexical specification, a non-initial UHT to any syllable which is not immediately adjacent to that containing the initial UHT.

What this signifies is that the non-initial UHT has to be assigned with a minimum of one syllable separating it from the syllable bearing initial UHT. The restriction on the non-initial UHT occurring on a syllable immediately adjacent to one bearing initial UHT does not apply to bisyllabic items. In two-syllable items with initial UHT on the first syllable, a non-initial UHT can occur on the immediately adjacent syllable. The first syllable with

UHT behaves like a sequence of two syllables with initial UHT on the first syllable when it comes to the application of the principle of non-adjacency. This fits in with our earlier observation that monosyllables with UHT would have come to be regarded by speakers as equivalent to two-syllable items with initial UHT on the first syllable. In keeping with our analysis, initial UHT on the second syllable does not behave in the same manner as when it occurs on the first syllable. Thus, in three-syllable items with initial UHT on the second syllable, the language does not allow for the second UHT to occur on the immediately adjacent third syllable.

What all this establishes is that the second syllable bearing initial UHT is not treated as if it were followed by an unrealised syllable for purposes of non-initial UHT assignment. The behaviour of initial UHT on the first and second syllables serves to confirm our earlier observations. The domain of the initial UHT is, in fact, the first two syllables, and any monosyllable bearing such a UHT is treated as if it were a two-syllable sequence. This ultimately owes its origins to syllabic restructuring and the resulting reinterpretation of word initial stress as UHT.

Let us now examine some examples of lexical items in GC. Firstly, we will look at some monosyllabic items with UHT.

(56)　　Monosyllabic Items With Underlying H-tone

a.	míi		"I, me, my" (emphatic)
b.	yúu		"You, your" (emphatic)
c.	híi		"He, him, his" (emphatic)
d.	wíi		"We, us, our" (emphatic)
e.	dée ~	dém	"they, them, their" (emphatic)
f.	fúl		"full"
g.	gú		"go"
h.	kyán		"can" (noun)
i.	bóz		"buzz"
j.	bín		"bin"
k.	dá		"that"

l. wán ~ wáan   "one"
m. gí   "give"
n. bón   "burn"

Let us, at this stage, identify the conventions which will be used for marking tone in GC. As in the items above, the presence of a UHT which has surfaced will be represented by the symbol ´ above the first element in the nucleus of the syllable involved. In syllables with reduced UHT, the symbol employed will be `. Syllables with no UHT will be left unmarked.

It is clear from our analysis so far that monosyllabic items of the type presented above carry initial UHT on their first and only syllable. From the point of view of their tonal specification, therefore, they are identical to items of more than one syllable bearing initial UHT on the first syllable and without a second UHT. We will now look at a set of examples of such items.

(57) Items With Sole Underlying H-tone On First Syllable

a. prójuus   "Guyana Marketing Corporation"
b. fárin   "foreign"
c. kálik   "colic"
d. bégin   "begging"
e. gáilain   "queue for scarce commodities"
f. kámanis   "indecency"
g. ániimal   "animal"
h. ránggatang   "ruffian"
i. báchila   "bachelor"
j. árdinerii   "ordinary"
k. kómfatebl̩   "comfortable"

In contrast to the monosyllabic items with UHT presented in (56), there are items of one syllable without UHT. A sampling of these is presented below.

(58) **Monosyllabic Items Without Underlying H-tone**

a.	mi	"I, me" (unemphatic)
b.	yu	"You, your" (unemphatic)
c.	ii	"He, him, his" (unemphatic)
d.	wi ~ wii	"We, us, our" (unemphatic)
e.	de ~ dem	"they, them, their" (unemphatic)
f.	fu	"for, to"
g.	gu ~ gun ~ gwain	future marker
h.	kyan	"can" (modal)
i.	doz	iterative marker
j.	bin ~ did	past tense marker
k.	a	continuative aspect marker
l.	wan	indefinite article
m.	di	definite article
n.	pon	"on"

From our analysis, monosyllabes without UHT are part of the same tonal class as items of more than one syllable with initial UHT on the second syllable. What follows is a listing of some items of more than one syllable with their only UHT, the initial UHT, falling on the second syllable.

(59) **Items With Sole Underlying H-tone On Second Syllable**

a.	projúus	"(to)produce"
b.	tudée	"today"
c.	kalék	"collect"
d.	biigín	"begin"
e.	tumára	"tomorrow"
f.	riisíiva	"(kitchen) sink"
g.	agáma	"lizard"
h.	amériika	"America"
i.	priizómshosnis	"presumption"
j.	gumárabiik	"gum arabic"

With the reinterpretation of word initial stress as UHT the maximum number of UHTs allowed per item moved from one to two. The introduction of an initial UHT occurred right across the board for all items with a non-initial UHT on the third syllable or later. Items which originally had UHT on the second syllable would not have been affected. Word initial stress would, in these cases, have been reduced by the stress associated with the immediately adjacent UHT. In the examples below, stress occurring as a feature quite independent of tone is marked by ' immediately before the stressed syllable.

(60) **Reinterpretation Of Word Initial Stress As UHT**

English Cognate	Before Stress Reinterpretation	After Stress Reinterpretation
under'stand	'andastáan	àndastáan
Portu'guese	'potagí	pòtagí
masque'rade	'maskaréed	màskaréed
enter'tain	'entatéen	èntatéen
bothe'ration	'badaréeshan	bàdaréeshan
edu'cation	'ediikéeshan	èdiikéeshan
auto'matic	'atamátik	àtamátik
recommen'dation	'rekamendéeshan	rèkamendéeshan

The reinterpretation of word initial stress as UHT meant that in modern GC, initial UHT had to be assigned to either the first or second syllable. This is the substance of the rule presented in (54). The first two syllables had become the domain of the initial UHT. We have already observed that monosyllabic items with UHT came to be treated by speakers in the same way as were two-syllable items with UHT on the first syllable. These items were regarded as possessing an unrealised second syllable.

Simultaneously, another feature developed in modern GC as a result of the reinterpretation of word-initial stress as UHT. The language began to allow two UHTs per item. Because of the new possibilities available to monosyllables with UHT, the initial syllable carrying UHT in a two-syllable item could function as if it were itself a sequence of two syllables with UHT on the first one. If an additional UHT were added to the final syllable of the item, the presence of the unrealised second syllable would have satisfied the conditions for the application of the rule in (55). This rule blocks the occurrence of UHTs on adjacent syllables within the same item. The result of all this was that though two-syllable items with two UHTs had become possible within the language, no such items existed.

The gap was filled by the addition of a UHT on to the second syllable of some items which already bore initial UHT on the first syllable. Below is presented a list of some of these items.

(61)	English Cognate	Before UHT Addition	After UHT Addition
'window	wínda	wìndá
'water	wáata	wàatá
'motor	móotoo	mòotóo
'fairy	féerii	fèeríi
'paddy	pádii	pàdíi
'cotton	kátn̩	kàtń̩
'bottle	báatl̩	bàatĺ̩
'wallet	wálit	wàlít
'market	máakit	màakít
'rubbish	róbish	ròbísh
'lizard	lízad	lìzád
'plantain	plántin	plàntín

Other two-syllable words with UHT on the first syllable did not go through the process of second UHT addition. Below are some of these.

(62)	English Cognate	GC Item
'feather	féda
'butter	bóta
'gallows	gyáloos
'hurry	hórii
'happy	hápii

'mutton	mótn
'label	léebl
'mallet	málit
'hatchet	háchit
'punish	pónish
'gizzard	gízad

Evidence exists for our proposal that the class of two-syllable items with two UHTs represents an innovation in modern GC. There are a number of Djuka items with UHT on the first syllable which have two-syllable GC cognates with two UHTs. If modern Djuka, as we have argued, is similar to what proto-GC was like, the second UHT in each of these items must have developed in modern GC. Below are some examples of Djuka items with UHT on the first syllable and their modern GC cognates with two UHTs.

(63)	Djuka Item	Modern GC Item	Gloss
	bóbi	bòbíi	"breast"
	sábi	sàbíi	"know"
	dóti	dòtíi	"earth"
	hébi	hèbíi	"heavy"
	tóli	stòríi	"story"
	báka(r)a	bàkrá	"whiteman"
	gwána	gwàaná	"iguana"

The addition of a second UHT in modern GC only affected some two-syllable items with UHT on the first syllable. One would, therefore, expect that there would also exist in modern GC two-syllable items which were tonally identical to Djuka cognates with UHT on the first syllable. This is indeed so as is demonstrated by the examples in (64) below.

(64)	Djuka Item	Modern GC Item	Gloss
	wéli	wéerii	"tired"
	sébiṇ	sévṇ	"seven"
	fája	fáya	"fire"

sísa	sísta	"sister"
líba	ríva	"river"
úman	úman	"woman"

The main impact of the introduction of second UHTs on two-syllable items already possessing UHT on the first syllable has been on morphologically complex items. This is an issue which will be dealt with in the next section. What we are going to examine here are some of the limited number of mono-morphemic minimal pairs which were produced. These are presented below in (65).

(65) **Minimal Pair**   Gloss

a. pákit   "packet"
   pàkít   "pocket"

b. rákit   "racket"
   ràkít   "rocket, racquet"

c. píla   "pillar"
   pìlá   "pillow"

d. flówa   "flour"
   flòwá   "flower"

e. báara   "borrow"
   bàará   "kind of peas cake"

f. léta   "letter to someone"
   lètá   "letter of the alphabet"

g. tórkii   "Turkey"
   tòrkíi   "turkey"

The analysis adopted in this section allows us to explain a particular phenomenon which would otherwise appear puzzling. Certain three-syllable items with their sole UHT on second syllable have two-syllable variants with two UHTs. These variant forms were produced historically by the deletion of the first syllable in the three-syllable items. This produced two-syllable items with UHT on the first syllable. UHT addition then applied to the two-syllable variants thus produced. Below are some examples.

(66)	Three Syllable Variant	Two Syllable Variant	Gloss
	awáara	wàará	"fruit name"
	anánsii	nànsíi	"Anansii"
	babéejan	bèeján	"Barbadian"

We have presented evidence that, in two-syllable items with two UHTs, the first syllable is regarded by speakers as being followed by an unrealised second syllable. This allows the second UHT to appear on the final syllable without violating the principle that two UHTs should not appear on immediately adjacent syllables. We have also argued that two-syllable items with two UHTs originated in proto-GC forms with the sole UHT on the first syllable. If one counts the unrealised syllable, the second UHT was added in modern GC to the third syllable. Support for this can be found in what has happened to certain proto-GC items of more than two syllables with the sole UHT on the first syllable. Some of these items but not others have received an additional UHT in modern GC. In all such cases where UHT addition has occurred, the new UHT has appeared on the third syllable. This would be, according to our analysis, exactly the same syllable to which it has been added in equivalent two-syllable items. What we are clearly, therefore, dealing with is the same process of UHT addition, whether in items of two syllables or longer. The process had its origins in two-syllable items triggering off UHT-addition in the longer items. Below are presented some examples of items longer than two syllables with UHT addition.

(67) Three Syllable Items With UHT Addition

English Cognate	Before UHT Addition	After UHT Addition
'penalty	pénaltii	pènaltíi
'customer	kóstoma	kòstomá
'capital	kyápital	kyàpitál
'punishment	pónishment	pònishmént
'envelope	énviiloop	ènviilóop
'sacrifice	sákafais	sàkafáis
'alligator	áliigeeta	àliigéeta
'caterpillar	kyátapila	kyàtapíla
'agriculture	ágriikolcha	àgriikólcha
'commentator	kámenteeta	kàmentéeta

2.3 The Tonal Morphology Of Modern GC

The most conservative Afro-English Creole varieties such as Saramaccan, Djuka and Sranan have a very restricted derivational morphology. Almost the only process of word formation which exists in these languages is compounding. The influence of English on modern GC has served to introduce a limited number of derivational morphemes into the language. With the evolution of the tonal system, an interesting interaction has developed between tone and the segmental derivational morphological system of the language. In fact, every use of tone within the morphological system involves the presence or absence of a second UHT within an item. Since, as we have been arguing, second UHTs did not exist in the earliest stages of the language, this use of tone must be a relatively new feature.

The first, and perhaps the most basic morphological use to which tone has been put is in marking the vocative. In two-syllable nicknames derived from lexical items with their sole UHT on the first syllable, a second UHT is added. However, this tonal pattern is used not only when nicknames are used to address people, but to refer to them in their absence. What was originally a vocative morphological device has become extended to being a marker of items used as personal names. Below are some examples.

(68)   Minimal Pair   Gloss

    a.   láiyan   "lion"
        làiyán   "nickname"

    b.   táiga   "tiger"
        tàigá   "nickname"

    c.   kápa   "copper"
        kàpá   "nickname"

    d.   pórpl   "purple"
        pòrpĺ   "nickname"

    e.   móstad   "mustard"
        mòstád   "nickname"

Some family names have their sole UHT on the first syllable. However, no two-syllable first names with UHT on the first syllable are allowed without an additional UHT. It can be argued that it is by the first name that someone is more likely to be addressed in face-to-face interaction. If one accepts this, it is easy to understand that a second UHT originally marking vocative becomes extended to morphologically mark the class of first names. The use of second UHTs in two-syllable first names produces minimal pairs or near minimal pairs such as the following.

(69)   Last Name   First Name

    hénrii   (Henry)   hènríi   (Henry)
    déevid   (David)   dèevíd   (David)
    édwadz   (Edwards)   èdwád   (Edward)
    ándruuz   (Andrews)   àndrúu   (Andrew)
    wílyamz   (Williams)   wìlyám   (William)

sámwelz   (Samuels)   sàmwél   (Samuel)
fílips   (Phillips)   fìlíp   (Phillip)

In spite of the impression which might be created by the above, many two syllable family names with UHT on the first syllable also have a second UHT, e.g. /àlíi/ "Ali", /sànkóo/ "Sancho", /pàndée/ "Panday", /hàrís/ "Harris", etc. This can produce a minimal pair as in /tèelá/ "Taylor" vs. /téela/ "tailor". What all of this is aimed at establishing is the basic vocative and naming functions of the second UHT.

In a certain number of two syllable words with UHT on the first syllable, the addition of a UHT to the final syllable has come to be employed as a morphological device. In the following pairs of items, the item with the sole UHT on the first syllable appears to be the basic term, the root, representing a literal family relationship. The other item, with an additional UHT on the second syllable, represents an institutional relationship or position.

(70)   Minimal   Gloss
        Pair

   a.   móda   "mother, i.e. female parent"
        mòdá   "female head of religious order
                    or organisation"

   b.   fáada   "father, i.e. male parent"
        fàadá   "priest"

   c.   sísta   "sister, i.e. female sibling"
        sìstá   "female member of religious
                    order or organisation;
                    nursing sister"

   d.   bróda   "brother, i.e. male sibling"
        bròdá   "male member of religious order
                    or organisation"

The question arises as to the reason why the second

UHT came to signal the "organisational" meaning in the above examples. The answer may lie in the extension of the use of the second UHT employed in the vocative. It was a short step for speakers to take, to start using the second UHT for items which referred to persons who were called /bròdá/, /sìstá/, /mòdá/, etc. in face-to-face interaction but who were not family relations.

The use of the second UHT as a morphological device operates elsewhere in the language. In a small class of two-syllable items, roots with the sole UHT on the first syllable signal a general meaning. The derived forms with the second UHT represent a more restricted or specific aspect of the meaning expressed in the root. This would be in keeping with the basic vocative-type function of the second UHT as a derivational morpheme. The restricted or specific meanings signalled by the use of the second UHT in the items below could have been perceived by speakers as being more familiar. This familiarity would, in turn, have been related in their minds to the vocative. This analysis would work for the first four pairs of items presented in (71) below. However, in the fifth pair, it is the item with the second UHT which has the more general meaning.

(71)   **Minimal Pair**   **Gloss**

a. práblem   "problem"
   pràblém   "a mathematics problem"

b. ánsa   "answer, response"
   ànsá   "written answer in a school situation"

c. dótii   "physically or morally dirty"
   dòtíi   "physically dirty"

d. nástii   "physically or morally nasty"
   nàstíi   "physically nasty"

	e.	léedii	"lady-like female"
		lèedíi	"woman"

The segmental derivational morphemes which appeared in modern GC as a result of influence from English were all suffixes. One of these was /-ii/ "approximating a particular quality". This morpheme frequently occurred with one-syllable or two-syllable roots carrying UHT on the first syllable. Many of the items produced as a result of the use of the suffix were subject to the second UHT addition which was sweeping the language. The position of the suffix as the second or third syllable meant that second UHT was being added to the syllable the suffix occupied. Because of the frequency with which this happened, speakers began to perceive the suffix as itself possessing UHT. It is thus that we would reconstruct the development of /-ii/ as a derivational suffix possessing UHT. The morpheme /-ii/ must have come into the language right at the time when second UHT addition was just beginning to occur. The reason for concluding this can be seen in the last four examples (i-l) in (72) below. Even though the roots involved have a second UHT, /-ii/ combines with these roots as if they possessed first syllable UHT only.

(72)

	Root	Suffix	Word	Gloss
a.	sáaf	-íi	sàafíi	"softish"
b.	wét	-íi	wètíi	"wettish"
c.	réd	-íi	rèdíi	"reddish"
d.	kóol	-íi	kòolíi	"coldish"
e.	plástik	-íi	plàstikíi	"plastic-like"
f.	chúpid	-íi	chùpidíi	"silly"
g.	pépa	-íi	pèpa(r)íi	"peppery"
h.	pórpl	-íi	pòrplíi	"purplish"
i.	ròbísh	-íi	ròbishíi	"rubbish-like"
j.	yèlá	-íi	yèla-íi	"yellowish"
k.	pèepá	-íi	pèepa(r)íi	"papery"
l.	àrínj	-íi	àrinjíi	"orangeish"

A more English-influenced morpheme /-ish/ operates

as a variant of /-ii/ in GC. The segmental features of /-ii/ are strongly associated with the more conservative Creole varieties. The use of /-ísh/ as a substitute has left the tonal properties of the more conservative variant very much intact. The result is that /-ish/ possesses UHT and, when attached to roots such as /réd/ and /yèlá/ produce /rèdísh/ and /yèla-ísh/.

There are other segmental derivational morphemes with UHT in modern GC. There is, for example, the suffix /-n̩/ which operates as a verb formant. It is attached to monosyllabic roots which have UHT. In combination with roots such as /stréet/ "straight", /háad/ "hard" and /sáaf/ "soft", the items /strèetń̩/ "make straight", /hàadń̩/ "make hard" and /sàafń̩/ "make soft" are produced. It seems likely that, as was the case with the morpheme /-ii/, the UHT associated with /-n̩/ developed as a result of UHT addition. Since /-n̩/ always appeared on the second syllable, the added UHT came to be regarded by speakers as a feature of the derivational morpheme rather than as simply the second UHT in a two-syllable item.

The two derivational morphemes /-ín/ "noun formant" and /-á/ "an instrument (as opposed to a human agent) carrying out an action" behave in rather similar ways. They both have UHT and this serves to contrast them with segmentally identical morphemes without UHT. These are /-in/ "continuative aspect marker" which occurs in more English-influenced varieties of GC, and /-a/ "a human agent carrying out an action". The addition of second UHTs and the resulting possibility of suffixes being able to bear UHT has produced differentiation between the two functions of the segmental sequence /-in/. The same has occurred for the segmental form /-a/. Let us now look at the examples involving /-in/ versus /-in/.

(73)   **The /-ín/ And /-in/ Morphemes**

	Item	Gloss
a.	pèentín	"(a) painting"
	péentin	"(verb) painting"
b.	sìngín	"singing practice"
	síngin	"(verb) singing"
c.	plèeín	"play, recreation"
	pléein	"(verb) playing"
d.	klìinín	"shoe polish"
	klíinin	"(verb) cleaning"
e.	kòlarín	"food dye"
	kólarin	"(verb) colouring"
f.	kòvarín	"(a) covering"
	kóvarin	"(verb) covering"

Below are some examples of the occurrences of the /-á/ versus /-a/ morphemes.

(74)   **The /-á/ And /-a/ Morphemes**

	Item	Gloss
a.	wàshá	"washing machine"
	wásha	"person who washes"
b.	skrèepá	"tool for scraping"
	skréepa	"someone who scrapes"
c.	prìntá	"instrument for printing"
	prínta	"a print worker"
d.	rìidá	"reader (text book)"
	ríida	"someone who reads"
e.	pàlishá	"mechanical polisher"
	pálisha	"someone who polishes"

There is a group of suffixes in English "-ate", "-fy", "-ize", "-ute" and "-ism". As is pointed out by Fudge (1984, pp.52-103), these morphemes assign stress two syllables before, when they are attached to bound roots. Cognate forms /-eet/, /-fai/, /-aiz/, /-yuut/ and /-izm/ occur in items which appear in certain varieties of GC showing some degree of English influence. When affixed to bound roots of two syllables, the English stress assigned by these suffixes would be on the first syllable. With this stress reinterpreted in GC as initial UHT, any addition of a second UHT would occur on the third syllable, the one bearing the suffix. It turns out that all of these derivational morphemes carry UHT. This is most likely the result of UHT addition, with this second UHT coming to be regarded as a feature of the morpheme occupying the third syllable in these items. We present some of the occurrences of these morphemes in GC in the following examples.

(75)   The Morphemes /-éet/, /-fái/, /áiz/, /-yúut/, /-ízm/

	English Cognate	GC Item
a.	'calculate	kyàlkyuléet
b.	'imitate	ìmiitéet
c.	'demonstrate	dèmanstréet
d.	com'municate	komyùuniikéet
e.	'satisfy	sàtisfái
f.	'magnify	màgniifái
g.	'terrorize	tèraráiz
h.	'realise	rèeyaláiz
i.	dis'organize	dìsarganáiz
j.	'distribute	dìstribyúut
k.	'persecute	pòrsiikyúut
l.	'contribute	kòntriibyúut

m.	'racialism	rèeshalízam
n.	'socialism	sòoshalízam
o.	im'perialism	impìiryalízam

What we have managed to establish in this section is that tone plays an active part in the derivational morphology of modern GC. In every case, it is the second UHT in the item which is involved. In addition, this UHT appears on syllables which bear no UHT in proto-GC nor stress in English cognates. It is clear that it was the process of UHT addition which had occurred in modern GC that created the conditions for the appearance of UHT on certain derivational suffixes. The question arises as to the nature of the tonal specification for these bound morphemes within the lexicon. It is being proposed here that each of the bound derivational morphemes which manifest the presence of UHT in GC is assigned the second UHT allowed within a root in the language. This permits items with one UHT to receive a derivational morpheme which is made up of or includes a second UHT. Roots with two UHTs already attached do not allow for the appearance of a third UHT. This can be seen, for example, in the behaviour of the vocative and related forms. In these cases, where the root already possesses two UHTs, e.g. /mònii/ "money", no additional UHT can appear in the derived form, e.g. /mònii/ "a nickname". When a suffix is involved such as the instrumental suffix /-á/ no UHT surfaces when it is attached to stems such as /jènaréet/ and /kyàlkaléet/ to produce /jènaréeta/ "generator" and /kyàlkaléeta/ "calculator". A suffix with UHT is really one which will receive the second UHT allowed to a root, if that UHT has not yet been assigned.

This has important implications for the tonal specifications of roots within the lexicon. Every such root can be said to possess two UHTs. The initial UHT is obligatorily associated with either the first or second syllable. The second UHT can occur on any subsequent non-contiguous syllable or may remain unassociated with any syllable in the root. When a suffix of the sort which can bear UHT is attached to a root possessing an unassociated second UHT, this UHT becomes realised on the suffix. The proposition being made here is that every root with an initial UHT also has a second UHT, whether it is associated with a following syllable or not. This fits in to our reconstruction of the transition from proto-GC to the modern form of the language. We argued that syllabic restructuring had resulted in items being allowed a maximum of two UHTs as compared with the single UHT previously permitted. The evidence we now have suggests that the introduction of the second UHT was not an optional one affecting only some roots. Rather, it affected all roots which possessed a UHT. The second UHT simply remained unassociated in some roots.

There is the case of a certain class of three-syllable word ending in /-a/. The ending in the English cognates is /-ə/. Speakers of GC, faced with a large number of borrowings from English, would have noticed that the syllable containing the ante-penultimate mora was the one which tended to be marked for prominence in the source language. There is the English rule for assigning stress in mono-morphemic items ending in syllables made up of one mora, which would include /-ə/. This places stress on the syllable containing the ante-penultimate mora. (Fudge, 1984, p.29) However, when the /-ə/ ending is used to represent the agentive morpheme in English, and is attached to a bound root, stress is placed on the ante-penultimate syllable. (Fudge, 1984, p.70) I would propose that, when the /-ə/ morpheme occurred attached to a bound root, GC speakers would have been unable to recognise the item as bi-morphemic. There would be little to differentiate these for non-speakers of English from many mono-morphemic words in English which end in /-ə/, e.g. "replica", "bachelor", "cinema", etc.

What would be the implications of treating all cases of /-ə/ endings on bound roots in English as mono-morphemic? In items with a penultimate syllable containing one mora, the syllable containing the ante-penultimate mora would be the ante-penultimate syllable. It would be this syllable which would be marked for prominence, the same syllable as would have been marked if the final /-ə/ had been treated as the agentive morpheme, e.g. " 'coroner", " 'sorcerer", " 'usurer", etc. However, when the penultimate syllable contains two moras, treating the item as mono-morphemic would produce prominence on the penultimate syllable, since it contains the ante-penultimate mora. Treating the item as having an agentive suffix /-ə/ would result, on the other hand, in stress being assigned to the ante-penultimate syllable. In the following items where the penultimate syllable /-sin-/ or /-nis-/ contains two moras, stress is nevertheless assigned to the ante-penultimate syllable as a result of the agentive /-ə/ suffix, e.g. " 'passenger", " 'messenger", " 'minister", " 'banister", etc. There is only one way that all the occurrences of word-initial prominence could be predicted in /-a/ final three-syllable items which do not contain a free root and which, therefore, are regarded as consisting of one morpheme. This would involve not counting the final syllable, i.e. treating it as if it were not a separate syllable. This is a rule which, we would argue, GC speakers applied to such items as they were borrowed from English. Furthermore, according to Fudge (1984, p.38, p.92), there are certain three-syllable mono-morphemic items in English ending in the vowel /-ə/, e.g. " 'cylinder", " 'ancestor", which speakers of English need to treat as not having a final syllable in order to assign stress correctly. This would have reinforced what was already naturally happening within GC as it borrowed large numbers if items from English.

One might very well ask whether all of this is really part of the perception of a GC speaker. Might such a speaker not simply know which syllable is assigned UHT in the lexicon of his language, without noticing that there was any generalisation that could be made about UHT placement? The fact that word stress is predictable in a large number of

English words would not have been lost on GC speakers. The location of one UHT in every item of English origin is on the same syllable as that stressed in English. Thus, English stress placement rules could, in a limited way, have been converted to UHT placement rules in GC.

UHT addition in three-syllable items which end in /-a/ and do not contain a free root provide evidence for this proposal. In such items, English assigns stress to the first syllable, either because (i) of the presence of the agentive suffix /-a/, (ii) the penultimate syllable is made up of only one mora and, therefore, does not contain the ante-penultimate mora, or (iii) the final syllable containing /-a/ does not count for the purposes of stress assignment. When these items are borrowed into GC, the stress on the first syllable becomes reinterpreted as initial UHT on the first syllable. There is, thus, the possibility of a second UHT being added to the third syllable in some such items. In fact, however, when a second UHT is added in this type of item, it appears on the second syllable. As we have noted in the previous section, second UHT addition only occurs on the second syllable when that syllable is word final. This suggests that the final syllable ending in /-a/ is not regarded as a syllable for purposes of assigning the second UHT. It is particularly significant that second UHT addition on the second syllable of these items is not restricted to words of English origin. This treatment, originally introduced as a means of predicting initial UHT placement in words of English origin, had become generalised to any /-a/ final three-syllable item with UHT on the first syllable, regardless of origin. Some /-a/ final three-syllable items with second UHT on the second syllable are presented below.

(76) /-a/ Final Three-Syllable Items With Second UHT — Gloss

bànísta	"banister"
mìnísta	"minister"
rèjísta	"register"
pàsínja	"passenger"
mèsínja	"messenger"
mànínja	"manager"
kyàarpínta	"carpenter"
kyàríkta	"character"
àafísa	"officer"
jànίta	"janitor"
fòrnícha	"furniture"
vìnίiga	"vinegar"
shèrίiga	"a fresh-water crab"
òobίiya	"obeah, witchcraft"
bàrtíka	"Bartica, place name"

There is a small number of /-a/ final three-syllable items which have UHT on the first syllable and which have second UHT on the third syllable. The items /làmitá/ "clumsy person", /wàlabá/ "a variety of wood", and /kòstomá/ "customer" make up an almost exhaustive list.

Whenever /-a/ final three-syllable items with UHT on the first syllable occur as personal names, particularly first names, they must take a second UHT on a following syllable. This is in keeping with our previous observations about the use of second UHTs to mark the vocative and personal names in GC. Interestingly, the second UHT is added to the second syllable. This is in keeping with our observation that, in such three-syllable items, the final syllable is not treated as if it existed. Below are some examples.

(77) /-a/ Final Three-   Gloss
      Syllable Names With
      Second UHT

màníka	"Monica"
jèníifa	"Jennifer"
ànjíla	"Angela"
jèsíika	"Jessica"
àlíva	"Oliver"
kwàmína	"Quamina"
kwàshíba	"Quasheba"

Fudge (1984, p.38, p.92) makes the point that the English items "cylinder" and "ancestor" have the underlying phonological forms /silindr/ and /ansestr/ in which the final /r/ is non-syllabic. He does this in order to explain the fact that both these items receive stress on the first syllable in English. He uses as supporting evidence the adjectival forms of these items, i.e. "cylindrical" and "ancestral", to imply that the final syllabic /ə/ is a low level phonological substitution for the non-syllabic /r/ when the latter occurs in word-final position.

The evidence from GC is that speakers may very well have acquired from English a perception that word-final /-a/ is non-syllabic in three-syllable items. They may, in turn, have applied this to a much larger number of occurrences than is the case in English. This is supported by the fact that GC treats three-syllable items ending in /-l/ and /-al/ in the same as it does those ending in /-a/. If /-a/ is regarded as an /r/ substitute in these items, it is not surprising that items ending in the other alveolar liquid in the language, either in its syllabic form or preceded by /a/, would be treated in the same way. When three-syllable /-l/ or /-al/ final items with UHT on the first syllable have a second UHT placed on a following syllable, it is the second syllable which receives it. These endings, like /-a/, are treated in these items as if they were underlyingly non-syllabic. Significantly, syllabic nasals which exist in GC do not receive the same treatment.

(78) /-l/ & /-al/ Final   Gloss
      Three-Syllable Items
      With Second UHT

    bàisíkl̩   "bicycle"
    spèktíkl̩(z)   "spectacles"
    àrtíkl̩   "article"
    hàaspítal   "hospital"

2.4 Tone Group Rules

Words in GC sentences are grouped into units within which the tonal shape of individual lexical items is modified. Only the final UHT within the unit is able to surface. As we shall argue, this modification is the result of the words within the unit being treated tonally as if they were a single lexical item. The closeness of the syntactic and/or semantic links among lexical items is employed in GC to group these items into units within the sentence. These units we shall refer to as tone groups.

An initial UHT coexisting with another UHT is subject to reduction at both the word and tone group levels. This transfer of tone reduction rules from the word level to that of the tone group often produces a clash. On one hand, there are the potential tone group units which would be created by applying the criterion of syntactic and/or semantic inter-relatedness amongst the various items. On the other hand, there are those sequences which, while satisfying this criterion, would require the reduction of a non-initial UHT in order to operate as a tone group. Where such clashes occur, syntactic and/or semantic factors are over-ridden by the requirement that the second UHT in an item cannot be reduced.

(79) Tone group boundary assignment rule

Assign tone group boundary

    a. At the end of syntactic units, e.g. the NP and the Verbal Complex, or after semantic units, i.e. compounds, and

    b. after any item within a sequence described in (a) which possesses a UHT which cannot be reduced, i.e. a second UHT.

The reason why there are two different criteria for assigning tone group boundaries lies in the link between the word and the tone group. The tone group, because it is made up of a set of syntactically or semantically inter-dependent items, is treated as if it were a single lexical item. In a single lexical item, the only UHT which is allowed to be reduced is the initial one. Thus, in a tone group made up of more than one item, a tone group boundary will have to be imposed immediately after an item with two UHTs. This is because the second UHT in individual words is not allowed to be reduced. At the level of the tone group, the special character of the second UHT is respected.

Let us examine how these tone group boundary assignment rules operate in practice. The tone group boundary will be marked in examples by #.

(80) **Tone group boundary assignment in sentences**

  a. di òol kyáar # dé # àndá # di bàtam hóus #
     "The old car is in the area underneath the house"

  b. nóf # chùpidíi # píipḷ # bìn bóut # hée # fràidii náit #
     "Many stupid people were around here on Friday night"

  c. di léta # dé # ìn di pòrpḷ ènviilóop # pòn di tèebḷ #
     "The letter is in the purple envelope on the table"

d. dèm doz láik # fu ték # wá # dèm kud gét #
"They like to take what they can get"

e. jáan-dem # gon kóm # tamàra náit #
"John and the others will come tomorrow night"

One observation which can be made from the above examples, is that mono-syllabic items without UHT are not allowed to be followed by a tone group boundary. The result is than any such item simply becomes part of the tone group which it precedes. This is what, for example, occurs with the item /di/ in the two tone groups within which it appears in (a). Another feature worth noting is the reduction of the initial UHT in items such as /óol/ in (a), /fráidii/ in (b), /pórpl̩/ in (c), and /tamára/ in (e). These are the only UHTs which can be reduced within a tone group. Compare this with the sequence /chùpidii píipl̩/ in (b). From a syntactic and semantic point of view, this is potentially a single tone group comparable to /òol kyáar/, /tamàra náit/, etc. However, the presence of a second UHT on /chùpidii/ meant that such a treatment was not going to be possible since non-initial UHTs cannot be reduced.

There is additional support for the view that tone rules operating at the word level are being applied at the level of the tone group. This is demonstrated in the examples below.

(81) Individual Items | | Tone Group Combinations

a. búk + kóva   buk kóva#
   "book" "cover" "book cover"

b. háad + pláastik   haad pláastik#
   "hard" "plastic" "hard plastic"

c. réd + pépa   red pépa#
   "red" "pepper" "red pepper"

d.	sháp "shop"	+ pòtagíi "Portuguese"	shap pòtagíi# "shop-owning Portuguese"
e.	stóf "stuffed"	+ àliigéeta "alligator"	stof àliigéeta# "stuffed alligator"
f.	jáan "John"	+ àndasṇ́ "Anderson"	jaan àndasṇ́# "John Anderson"

In the left hand column in the above examples, the first of the individual items is monosyllabic, with a UHT lexically associated with the only syllable. The second individual item in each case begins with a UHT which is not word final since the items involved are not monosyllabic. When they occur in tone group combinations as presented in the right hand column of the examples above, the lexically assigned UHT in the mono-syllabic item is deleted.

The explanation for this UHT deletion is that this represents the superimposition of word-level tonal patterns on to the level of the tone group. No word in GC of more than two syllables, except for the special group of three syllable items ending in /-a/, /-l̩/ and /-al/, has two UHTs on syllables which are immediately adjacent to each other. At tone group level, a sequence of two UHTs on immediately adjacent syllables with the second UHT on a syllable which is not word-final, would run counter to the pattern established at word level. In order to bring the tone group into line with what is possible at the word level, a UHT deletion rule is applied to the first UHT in such a sequence. The deletion rule could be presented as in (82).

(82) Tone group UHT deletion rule

> Delete a lexically assigned UHT when followed by a UHT on an immediately adjacent non-word-final syllable.

We have all along argued that many features associated with the word have been applied to the tone group. Where this is particularly obvious is in the treatment of tone groups containing monosyllabic items which do not have lexically specified UHTs on their only syllable. Let us examine what occurs when a tone group boundary appears after a sequence not containing a lexically specified UHT. A UHT is inserted by the tone group on the last item. In addition, there is what happens whenever a sequence involving more than one syllable without lexically specified UHT appears at the beginning of a tone group. A tone group specified UHT is assigned to the first syllable in the sequence. The tone group UHT assignment rules could be presented as in (83).

(83) Tone group UHT assignment rule

a. Assign UHT to the last syllable of a tone group not containing an item possessing lexically specified UHT.

b. Assign UHT to a tone group initial syllable without UHT which is immediately followed by another syllable without UHT.

The application of (83)a ensures that every tone group has a UHT on the final item, irrespective of whether this UHT is assigned lexically or by the tone group.

This parallels the tonal pattern of individual lexical items in GC which all have a UHT. This includes those monosyllabic items without UHT on their only syllable which, as we have argued in 2.2, possess a UHT associated with an unrealised second syllable. At the same time (83)b ensures that, at the beginning of the tone group, there should be no more than one syllable without UHT. Again, this parallels the tonal patterns permissible in individual lexical items.

Let us examine with reference to language data, the way that the rules outlined in (83) operate in practice.

(84) Individual Items   Tone Group Combinations

a. dem + go + bii + fu + shi   dèm go bii fu shí#
"They will be for her"

b. yu + doz + kéch + mi   yù doz kéch # mi#
"You catch me"

c. húu + dís + kóm + fu   hú # dís # kóm # fú#
"Who has this come for?"

d. dem + gon + kóm   dèm gon kóm#
"They will come"

e. ii + in + di + mód   ìi in di mód#
"He is in the mud"

In (84)a, we see the application of both the rules presented in (83). The rule of (83)a is applied to the sequence, made up as it is entirely of items without lexically specified UHTs. The last item, /shi/, therefore receives a UHT assigned by the tone group. Simultaneously, at the beginning of the tone group, there is a sequence involving more than one syllable without UHT. The result is that Tone Group Assignment Rule (83)b applied, assigning a UHT to the item /dem/. In the sentence in (84)b, in the first of the two tone groups, it was the (83)b rule which applied. This assigned a tone group UHT to /yu/. In the second tone group, it was the rule in (83)a which applied, assigning a UHT to the final and, in this case, only item within the tone group. This same rule applied in the same way to the fourth tone group in (84)c. In the case of the examples in (84)d and (84)e, it was the (83)b rule which applied. Accordingly, /dem/ and /ii/ received a tone group UHT. In both these cases, these items occurred at the beginning of the tone group, and did not already possess a UHT. They were, in addition, followed immediately by a syllable without UHT.

In the case of two-syllable items with two UHTs, their behaviour in relation to tone groups is quite variable. Because they possess two UHTs, for such items to occur within a tone group in a position where the second UHT in the item is not the final one, would be impossible. This is because, as has already been stated, the reduction of non-word-initial UHTs is not permissible within the tone group. However, some two-syllable items with two UHTs seem to be able to occur followed by another UHT in the same tone group. They are, however, treated as if they had only a single UHT, that on the first syllable. What this suggests is that the original his-torical tonal shape of these items is being resorted to. The effect is that only the UHT on the first syllable has to be reduced. The other is regarded as not existing for purposes of the operation of the UHT reduction rule within the tone group. Which two-syllable items with two UHTs in GC are allowed to behave in this fashion appears to be entirely arbitrary. In the examples presented in (85), we attempt to demonstrate the apparent randomness with which some two-syllable items possessing two UHTs are selected for this treatment and others excluded. The underlined two-syllable items in the examples below all possess two lexically assigned UHTs. However, those in the left-hand column are treated, for purposes of their association with the following item, as if they possessed only one UHT, that on the first syllable. The underlined items in the right-hand column do not receive this treatment.

(85) **Treated As Having UHT On First Syllable Only**   **Treated As Having Two UHTs**

    a.   <u>pàkit</u> píis#   <u>bìskít</u> # tín#
        "pocket money"   "biscuit tin"

    b.   <u>wàata</u> kyán#   <u>pèepá</u> # báag#
        "water can"   "paper bag"

    c.   <u>bèlii</u> péen#   <u>chàiníi</u> # máan#
        "belly pain"   "Chinese man"

d. stòorii búk#   àantíi # máan#
    "story book"   "effeminate man
                           (lit. aunty man)"

e. bòkit fúl#   bìskít # tín#
    "bucketful"   "biscuit tin"

For the most part, a particular two-syllable item with two UHTs will behave either like one or the other set of items above. Only rarely do we find an item within the language which will behave in one way in some close syntactic or semantic combinations, and in the other way in other combinations.

When two-syllable items with two UHTs occur as the final item in a tone group combination, preceded by another item with lexically specified UHT, these items are usually treated as if they had only one UHT, that on the first syllable. The difference with the items in the left-hand column of (85) is that this behaviour is not lexically restricted. Any two-syllable item with two UHTs will behave in this way. The underlined items in the examples below all possess two lexically assigned UHTs, even though they appear within the tone group combinations with a UHT on the first syllable only.

(86)   **Individual Items**   **Items In Tone Group**

a. léf + pàkít   lef pákit#
                             "left pocket"

b. shúga + bìskít   shùga bískit#
                             "sugar biscuit"

c. fáya + wàatá   fàya wáata#
                             "sulphuric acid
                             (lit. fire water)"

d. yèlá + pèepá   yèla péepa#
                             "yellow paper"

e. áyan + bòkít   àyan bókit#
                      "iron bucket"

f. chìkín + kòríi   chìkin kórii#
                      "chicken curry"

All the examples above involve the use of the one-UHT variant of the items with two UHTs when preceded by an item with a lexically specified UHT. Additional tone group rules are, however, at work in some of the examples. In (a), the lexical UHT associated with /léf/ is deleted because it is followed by a non-word-final UHT on an immediately adjacent syllable. This is the Tone Group UHT Deletion Rule presented in (82). In the examples (d) and (f) above, the additional process which occurs involves the non-final item in the tone group combination. Items such as /yèlá/ and /chìkín/ have two lexically specified UHTs. However, as observed in the discussion of the examples in (85), certain such items are permitted to behave as if they possessed only one UHT, that on the first syllable. This is allowed when, as in the examples (86) d & f, such items occur followed by an item with UHT which is a potential member of the same tone group.

In the tone group final items in (86) above, all function tonally as if they have a single UHT, one assigned to the first syllable. This is in spite of the fact that they have two lexically specified UHTs. What we see here seems to complement the observation we made when looking at the examples presented in (85). There seems to be a tendency for this type of item to revert back to its original proto-GC form when it occurs in certain positions within the tone group.

2.5 The Sentence Level

In many tone languages, the actual pitch at which a particular tone is realised is influenced by a phenomenon referred to in the literature as downdrift. Thus, successive tones become phonetically lower and lower in pitch until, at the end of the phrase or sentence, the high tones may be phonetically as low as or lower than the low tones which occurred at the beginning of the sentence. (Ohala, 1978, p.31) The phonetic facts of many tone languages point in the direction of tone assimilation as an explanation for downstep. In these languages, a tone sequence of H-L-H results in the second H being lower in pitch than the first. This is viewed as a case of the second H assimilating to the pitch of the preceding L-tone. (Hyman & Schuh, 1974, pp.84-85; Schuh, 1978, p.239; Clements, 1983, p.154)

The problem with downdrift in GC, however, is that it does not fit an analysis which proposes the lowering of an H-tone under the influence of an immediately preceding L-tone. When the first mora of a syllable receives a UHT, there is an immediate lowering in the pitch of the rest of the sentence, including any second mora within the same syllable. This applies recursively so that if a sentence possesses N number of undeleted UHTs, there will be N minus one cases of pitch lowering. The lowering occurs even when two UHTs are on immediately adjacent syllables and even immediately adjacent moras as in /gó ↓ dé/ "go there". In an example such as this, no L-tone has appeared between the first UHT and the downdrifted second one. An alternative analysis is needed.

Our proposal is in line with the alternative view of downdrift discussed by Schuh (1978, p.239). According to this view, downdrift is a natural, unmarked intonation motivated by some as yet unknown articulatory factor. By treating downdrift simply as an intonation pattern rather than as the result of the assimilation of H-tones to preceding L-tones, we are able to account for the phonetic facts of GC.

Unlike many of the tone languages in which downdrift has been observed, GC has no L-tones at the underlying level. Only H-tones exist at this level. This may explain the absence of an assimilatory type of downdrift. Our analysis of the downdrift in GC is that it is an intonational lowering applied to UHTs at sentence level.

Each UHT causes every following mora in the sentence to be realised at a pitch which is lower than it otherwise would have been. The UHT in a syllable where it occurs, is always associated with the first mora. Where a second mora exists within the syllable, this mora is also subject to the lowering effect of the UHT. This is to be expected since, as has been argued in 2.1 and 2.2, branching nuclei in GC are made up of two V-elements or moras. This means that such syllables have two peaks. Such an analysis would predict that two moras in a branching nucleus would differ in the phonetic pitch which they receive in a syllable with UHT. This is what actually occurs.

We need to construct a model which will predict surface pitch assignment at the sentence level. This model has to have as its input the tonal specifications which are a result of UHT assignment, reduction and deletion at word and tone group levels. There are three possible specifications which a syllable may have when it appears at the sentence level, (i) unreduced UHT, (ii) reduced UHT and (iii) zero tonal specification. In the case of (iii), an additional piece of information is necessary. This relates to whether it is located before or after the unreduced UHT within the tone group. All zero specified syllables occurring after an unreduced UHT within a tone group, receive a copy of the preceding UHT. The tone copying rule could read as follows.

(87) Unreduced UHT copying rule

> Copy an unreduced UHT on to every syllable to the right until the boundary of the tone group is reached.

We need to determine how, on the phonetic level, the distinction between the three underlying tonal specifications is signalled. The first distinction we have to deal with is that between syllables with unreduced UHT versus syllables with either of the other two possible specifications. We will assign a value 0 to the pitch of the unreduced UHT. By the tone copying rule in (87), this will copy on to any following moras within the same tone group. All other moras will have the pitch value -3. In the case of the distinction between those carrying UHT and those with no underlying tonal specification, the former trigger a pitch drop in all moras which follow. The latter, however, do not. We will assign a value of -1 to the pitch drop produced on the following moras in the sentence by the presence of a UHT on the first mora of a syllable. Let us examine how this works on an actual GC declarative sentence. # indicates the end of a tone group.

(88) mi fáada kòm hóom láang   "My father came
                                     home some time ago"

mi	fá	-ada	#	kò	-m	hó	-om	#	lá	-ang#	
-3	0			-3	-3	0			0		(From underlying specification)
		0 0					0			0	(Tone copying)
		-1 -1		-1	-2	-2	-3		-3	-4	(Lowering by -1 after each UHT)
-3	0	-1 -1		-4	-5	-2	-3		-3	-4	

We separated the syllables with branching nuclei in the above in moras, symbolized by the hyphen. We started out with the underlying tonal input symbolized by ´, `, and absence of a superscript over the first vowel of a syllable. With this as an input at the first stage, we assign the value of -3 to all the moras coming before the unreduced UHT within the tone group. The value 0 is attached to all moras bearing unreduced UHTs. At the second stage, tone copying takes place for those moras which occur after the unreduced UHT within the tone group. At the third stage, the pitch of each mora has the value -1 added to it for each UHT which precedes it. At the final level, by way of adding up all the pitch values for each mora, one is able to identify what its absolute pitch would be in the sentence. We attempt to represent this visually in (89) below.

(89)   mi fá -ada # kò -m hó -om # lá -ang#

         -3 0 -1 -1 -4 -5 -2 -3   -3 -4   (Actual pitch
                                              values)
    0   -
    1   - -
    2   -
    3   -   -
    4   -   -
    5   -

In the above, we notice a decline in pitch from the unreduced UHT associated with /fá-/ to that associated with /lá-/ Similarly, there is the absolute pitch of /-a/, the mora immediately following the first unreduced UHT, as compared with the much lower pitch of the mora /-ang/ which follows the last UHT. The decline in the absolute pitch of particular kinds of moras can also be seen if one compares the mora in /mi/ preceding the first unreduced UHT with that of the mora /-m/ preceding the second.

In a declarative sentence in GC, it is normally possible for the speaker to emphasise or focus on a particular item possessing an unreduced UHT. This is done by raising the pitch level of the moras in the syllable possessing the unreduced UHT by a value of +3 above what would otherwise be their pitch. We propose that such a syllable receives a UHT assigned by the sentence. The pitch of the first mora of a syllable with unreduced UHT is normally +3 relative to the mora immediately preceding it within the same tone group. This suggests that there is an extra UHT on a syllable already possessing an unreduced UHT which contributes the additional +3 to the pitch of the moras of that syllable. However, it should be pointed out that this additional UHT does not affect the pattern of downdrift in the moras of words which follow. Since the two UHTs are on the same syllable, the pitch of the moras of words following is calculated based on their having been preceded by a syllable with unreduced UHT. Let us examine how the emphatic UHT is inserted at sentence level in an actual sentence.

(90) mi FA -ada # ko -m ho -om # la -ang#

-3 0		-3	0		0	(From underlying specification)
0 0 0			-3	0	0	(Tone copying)
+3						(Emphatic sentence Level UHT)
	-1 -1	-1	-2	-2 -3	-3 -4	(Lowering by -1 after each UHT)
-3 +3	-1 -1	-4	-5	-2 -3	-3 -4	(Actual pitch values)

Most modern accounts of downstep in tone languages are based on the interaction between systematic downdrift and what are referred to as "floating tones". (Clements, 1983, pp.158-162) A floating tone is one which is not linked to a tone bearing unit. It, therefore, does not manifest itself on any segment within the sentence. However, a floating tone will participate in downdrift. Thus, in a language like GC, a floating UHT would reduce the pitch of those moras following in the sentence by a value of -1. Downstep is, therefore, downdrift which has occurred in the absence of the surface manifestation of the tone which would normally have triggered it. In negative declarative sentences in GC, there is downstep to the value of -1 starting with the first mora of the final tone group. We propose that this downstep is the product of a floating UHT in front of this tone group. This floating UHT is inserted at sentence level rather than at the lexical or tone group level. In the example below, downstep is marked by the use of the unreduced UHT symbol ´ before the mora to which the downstep applies. The pitch value in brackets represents unrealised pitch.

(91)   Jáan ín tíif ´ di rèd shót   "John didn't steal the red shirt"

```
Já -an # í -n # tí -if #  ´  di   rè -d   shó  -t#
 0  -1   -1 -2   -2 -3  (-3) -7   -7 -8   -5   -6
```

By interpreting downstep as involving a UHT without a tone bearing unit preceding the downstepped mora, we are able to fit downstep into the normal downdrift existing in GC sentences. The floating UHT causes the following mora in the syllable /di/ to be -7 instead of the -6 it would have been if not preceded by the floating tone. As a consequence, of course, all the following moras in the final tone group are themselves -1 relative to what their pitch would otherwise have been.

Downstep also occurs on the first mora of the final tone group in another kind of sentence. This is a sentence ending with a form of address operating as a sentence tag. Below are some examples.

(92)   Declarative Sentences With Address Tags.

   a. ìi doz kíl ´ máan   "It kills, man (address form)"
   b. mi móda nóo ´ mìsta jóonz   "My mother knows, Mr. Jones"
   c. yu héer di báai néem ´ kán   "You heard the boy's name, Khan"

Pitch assignment for the above sentences is presented in (93) below.

(93) a. ì -i do -z kí -l # ´ má -an#
        -3 -4 -4 -4 -1 -2 (-2) -3 -4

b. mi móda # nó -o # ´ mì -sta jó -onz#
    -3   0-1   -1 -2   (-2) -6 -7-7 -4 -5

c. yu hé -er # di bá -ai # né -em # ´ ká -n#
    -3 0 -1   -4 -1 -2   -2 -3   (-3) -4 -5

In the case of (93)a, the pitch drop in the second mora of the first item, /ii/, is the result of the Tone Group UHT Assignment Rule presented in (83)b. In relation to the downstep, this is analysed as involving, as with the negatives, a floating UHT inserted at sentence level in front of the final tone group. This produces a downdrift of -1 on the first syllable of the final tone group. The floating UHT having no mora with which to associate, is not realised on the surface. The result is that the downdrift on the first mora of the final tone group is perceived of as a downstep.

To conclude that downstep is indeed a distinctive feature in the tonal system of GC, we need only compare the three sentences in (92) with the following three.

(94) a. ìi doz kíl máan   "It kills, man"
     b. mi móda nóo mìsta jóonz "My mother knows Mr. Jones"
     c. yu héer di báai néem kán "You heard the boys's
                                  name is Khan"

In (94) above, with no downstep on the first mora of /máan/, /mista/ and /kán/, the sentences have quite different meanings from those in (92). The fact is that, apart from the presence of downstep on the first mora of the final tone group, the two sets of sentences have identical tonal specifications at the lexical and tone group levels. Downstep cannot be predicted, therefore, based on the tonal specifications introduced at either of these two levels. This supports our proposition that downstep is occurring as a result of the presence of a floating UHT introduced at sentence level in certain types of sentences but not others.

Let us now examine what occurs in 'Yes/No' questions in GC. The last mora in these sentences is subject to a pitch rise ending at a pitch +3 relative to that where it started. We propose that this pitch rise is the result of a sentence level UHT inserted at the end of the final tone group in the sentence. Since an unreduced UHT is always +3 relative to an immediately preceding mora in the same tone group, the floating UHT is assigned this pitch value. Since the floating UHT has no mora with which to associate, the effect of its presence is to induce a pitch rise of +3 over the duration of the immediately preceding mora. This is the source of the sentence-final pitch rise in a 'Yes/No' question such as that in (95) below. The pitch rise is represented by the symbol above the last mora of the sentence.

(95) dem gun ríich dé súun   "Will they arrive there early?"

      de -m gu -n rí -ich # dé # sú -un ´ #
      -3 -4 -4 -4 -1 -2   -2   -3 -4   -1

We have proposed a sentence-level floating UHT to explain the surface pitch configurations of (i) negative declarative sentences, (ii) declarative sentences with address tags, and (iii) 'Yes/No' questions. What is interesting is that only one floating UHT is allowed in any type of sentence in GC. Thus, in negative declarative sentences with address tags, only one floating UHT and consequently one downstep appears. This is illustrated in the example below.

(96) di hóus nó dón sél ´ báai   "Hasn't the house already been sold, boy?"

      di hó -us # nó # dó -n # sé -l # ´ # bá -ai#
      -3   0 -1   -1   -2 -3   -3 -4   -4   -5 -6

In the cases of negative "Yes/No" questions and "Yes/No" questions with an address tag, only one floating UHT appears. It is that associated with the question. The floating UHT appears at the end of the last tone group in the sentence, causing rising pitch on the last mora. This is illustrated in the examples in (97).

(97)

a. di bríiz # kyáan # kòm ín ´ #   "Can the breeze
not come in?"

di brí -iz # kyá -an # kò -m í -n ´ #
-3   0 -1   -1 -2   -5 -6 -3 -4 -1

b. dém # góot # doz dóon # gèt wée # gyól#   "Do those goats not
get away, girl?"

dé -m # gó -ot # do -z dó -on # gè -t wé -e # gyó -l ´ #
0 -1   -1 -2   -5 -5 -2 -3   -6 -7 -4 -5   -5 -6 -3

The floating UHT is assigned as an intonational device, i.e. it is a feature of GC sentence intonation. Only one can occur per GC sentence. This UHT performs a double function in negative declarative sentences with an address tag, causing single downstep at the beginning of the final tone group as in (96). Where negative sentences with an address tag are 'Yes/No' questions, the question function of the floating UHT is the one which takes precedence. The only sentence level deviation from predictable downdrift in this type of sentence is the rising pitch on the last mora of the sentence, marking question intonation.

There exists in GC a set of bisyllabic sequences whose tonal behaviour is extremely interesting. At the segmental level, the elements occupying the consonant and vowel slots of the first syllable are copied on to the consonant and vowel slots respectively of the second syllable. This is the case provided that one accepts a lexically restricted phonological rule which realises the consonant phoneme /h/ as [ʔ] in word-initial position. The alternative proposition, that /ʔ/ is realised as [h] between vowels is not as economical when one takes into account other aspects of the phonological system. In (98) below, we present the items.

(98) a. ʔehé   "Yes"
     b. ʔehé´   "Is that so?"
     c. ʔéʔé   "What is that!" (expression of surprise)
     d. ʔé´ʔé   "No"

We would argue that (98)a is the basic form from which the other three can be derived. From the tonal point of view, it possesses a single UHT which appears on the second syllable. In (98)b, what we have is the question intonation involving rising pitch on the last mora being induced by sentence final floating UHT. In (98)c, we have the two syllables, now each bearing UHT and belonging to separate tone groups. The explanation for this tonal pattern may lie in the behaviour of "Wh-" type questions in GC. They involve a "Wh-" type item such as /wích/ or /wá/ at the beginning of the sentence. These items have UHT and are not part of the following tone group. 'Wh-' type sentences have the downdrift pattern of declarative sentences. Below is an example of this kind of sentence.

(99)   wích sáid dem dé   "Where are they?"

        wí -ch # sá -id # de -m dé#
        0 -1   -1 -2   -5 -5 -2

Expressions of surprise can be regarded as essentially "Wh-" type questions. This is implied by the translation of (98)c. It is being suggested here that (98)c involves the appearance of a UHT on the first syllable paralleling that associated with /wích/ and /wá/. Consistent with the behaviour of the "Wh-"

type items, the syllable thus marked with UHT belongs to a separate tone group from the syllable which follows. It should be pointed out that this UHT on the first syllable is additional to the UHT on the second syllable which appears in (98)a.

In the case of the item in (98)d, we would argue that the first syllable becomes marked with UHT paralleling the UHT associated with all negative markers in GC, e.g. /ná/, /ín/, /kyáan/, /dóon/, etc. These markers never occur as part of the same tone group as items which follow in the sentence. Hence, the first syllable bearing the negative related UHT constitutes a separate tone group from the syllable which follows. This following syllable would continue to bear UHT consistent with the choice of (98)a as the basic form. Negative markers, when they occur in sentences, produce downstep as a result of a floating UHT inserted at sentence level immediately before the final tone group. This, we would argue, is exactly what happens in the case of (98)d. The result is that it receives downstep consistent with other negative declarative sentences in the language. This is demonstrated in (96) below.

(100)   ʔé # ˊ # ʔé   ===>   ʔé ˊ ʔé
          0   ˙1   ˙2

This analysis of items in (98) would apply equally well to a similar set of items which differ only in that they take a syllabic nasal as the segmental element occupying the vowel slot within the syllables.

(101)   ʔm̥hm̥   "Yes"
         ʔm̥hm̥ ˙   "Is that so?"
         ʔm̥ ʔm̥   "What is that!" (expression of surprise)
         ʔm̥ ˙ʔm̥   "No"

2.6 Supporting Evidence

The value of the analysis presented in Chap.2 is entirely dependent on two factors. The first of these is the accuracy of the observations made about the tonal system of Guyanese Creole (GC). Secondly, it would have to be demonstrated that the changes which have occurred to produce the tonal system of modern GC are not restricted to this language. It was claimed that these changes were triggered by phonological restructuring involving the introduction of branching nuclei into the language, a result of continued influence from English. A whole range of other Afro-English Creoles have themselves undergone such restructuring under the continued influence of English. It would have to be established that these too have developed tonal characteristics comparable to those in GC. The goal of this section is to examine the evidence on these two questions.

There has been work done before now on the role of tone in GC. Richard Allsopp (1972) provides the first systematic attempt to deal with this question. He focuses a lot of attention on two-syllable items with "... low-high pitch contour with stress on the first or low-pitched syllable". (p.111) These are the items which, according to our analysis, carry two UHTs, one on each syllable. The stress which he suggests occurs on the first syllable is for us a reduced UHT which causes a lowering in the pitch of the following mora(s) within the word. In an item with two moras in the first syllable, e.g. /wàatá/ "water", /bìskít/ "biscuit", the fall in pitch first affects the second mora of the first syllable. This pitch drop has the effect of making the syllable seem longer and more prominent. It is these phonetic facts which most likely led to Allsopp describing syllables with reduced UHTs as being stressed.

An important gap in Allsopp's approach is a failure to recognize that, in addition to "low-high" two-syllable items with "stress" on the first syllable, there were also "low-high" items without "stress" on the first syllable, e.g./aták/ "attack", /afóord/ "afford". These are items which we would describe as possessing a single UHT, the one appearing on the second syllable. This gap extends itself into his examination of three-syllable items. He fails to distinguish between those which have "low-high-high" tone patterns with "stress" on the first syllable, and those without "stress" on the first syllable. Thus, he does not capture the tonal distinction which exists in GC between /òobíiya/ "witchcraft" on one hand, and /riimémba/ "remember" on the other. For us, the former belongs to that special class of three-syllable item in which there are two lexically assigned UHTs, one on each of the first two syllables. These are the items in which the third syllable is treated as if it does not exist for purposes of the lexical assignment of UHT. The latter item for us has its sole UHT on the second syllable.

As a central theme of Allsopp's entire discussion of tone in GC is his conviction about two-syllable items with two UHTs, the items he refers to as "low-high" with stress on the "low" syllable. He feels that this tone pattern is the favourite and most basic one for two-syllable items. It is, for him, the pattern of all the older two-syllable words within the language, particularly those of African origin. He has a particular view of two-syllable items with its single UHT on the first syllable, the kind of items he describes as being marked by a "high-low" sequence. This sequence is, for him, the result of English influence and is associated with the more learned and non-folk vocabulary items within the language.

According to our historical reconstruction in 2.2, the tone pattern for items such as /wàatá/, involving as it does two UHTs, is a new tone pattern in GC. What is interesting in all this, therefore, is the fact that the new tonal pattern has become established on precisely those items which are oldest and with the strongest folk associations within the language. One explanation might very well be that it is these items which happened to be in the language at the time of the restructuring of proto-GC into modern GC. Thus, the newly developing tone pattern applied to large numbers of these items. Items borrowed subsequently from English had missed the spread of this new tone pattern and thus retained the older GC tone pattern produced by the straightforward conversion of English word-stress to UHT.

Allsopp (1972, p.116), by proposing the existence of word initial stress in an item like /kòkobé/ "leprosy", is describing in his own terms the reduced word-initial UHT which we argue exists in such items. He also observes that three-syllable verbs ending in /-eet/, /-ifai/, and /-aiz/ take high tone on the final syllable. This is very much in keeping with the observations made in 2.3.

The treatment by Allsopp of certain aspects of sentence intonation as well as /ʔehé/, /ʔm̩hḿ̩/ and related forms, provided an important starting point for the analysis presented in 2.5. More generally, the major difference between the observations made by Allsopp (1972) on tone in GC and that provided in this chapter has got to do with the theoretical tools employed. Enormous advances have been made in the study of tone languages in the last ten years or so, and this has made a great difference to what could now be achieved in an analysis of GC tone.

Another approach which accepts the tonal nature of GC is that of Berry (1976). He views GC as a pitch accent or tonal accent language with a maximum of one tonally accented syllable per item. Berry (1976, p.2, p.6) presents a schema for an unemphatic sentence with what he calls "fairly neutral" intonation. The schema shows downdrift of H-tones when preceded by L-tones. This, as we have seen in 2.5, would not account for the fact that in a sequence of two unreduced UHTs on immediately contiguous syllables, the second UHT is downdrifted relative to the first. Berry (pp.6-7) does accept that this occurs. He accounts for it by treating it as a case of "downstep" though he does not provide a precise definition of what he means by this term.

Holder (1972, 1978, 1984) concentrates his attention on Guyanese English rather than Guyanese Creole. However, at the level of prosody, these two language varieties are extremely similar. Maybe because he was working on a variety of English rather than a variety of Creole, Holder has restricted himself to using a stress-based approach. Holder's 1972 and 1978 work is mainly concerned with documenting Guyanese English deviations from the norms of stress placement in British English. In terms of our approach, what he is really examining is the addition of second UHTs on to items which, historically, had only one UHT, that on the initial syllable, e.g. "window", "appetite", "realise", "capitalism", etc.

Holder (1984) spells out in detail his notion of stress as it applies to Guyanese English. According to him, Guyanese English has a three-degree stress system. There is a strong up-beat, a strong down-beat and a weak beat. Holder (1984, p.2) goes on to state that "As this terminology suggests, primary stress is most often associated with high pitch, and secondary stress with low pitch; the difference between strong and weak beat is generally made by degree of loudness." This translates quite easily into our own three way system, that of unreduced UHT, reduced UHT and the absence of UHT specification. The difference between a syllable with UHT and one without is that the first mora in a syllable with UHT causes the mora following to downdrift.

The main focus of Holder (1984) is on stress rules which govern the ability of Guyanese English items to join together in compounds. What he discusses covers a large area of our analysis of tone group rules in 2.4.

Carter (1987) is the most modern and sophisticated study of tone in GC done so far. It presents GC as a ditonemic system involving an opposition between High and Low tones at both the underlying and surface levels. Given the theoretical differences between the approach of Carter and that taken in the present work, her conclusions agree in most respects with those expressed earlier in this chapter. One major difference is that, like Berry and Allsopp before her, she fails to distinguish between items such as /aták/ and /afóord/ with their first UHT on the second syllable, and those such as /wàatá/ and /bìskít/ with a UHT on each of the first two syllables. In addition, she incorrectly analyses the GC phonological system as involving no phonemic vowel length. The result is that she misses being able to identify the origin of the second UHT on the second syllables of items such as /wàatá/ and /bìskít/, an issue which was a major focus of her paper.

In this brief discussion, we have been able to survey the work of four writers who have dealt with the tonal properties of Guyanese language varieties from different perspectives. The analysis of GC tone presented in Chap. 2 may have taken a different theoretical approach but is clearly addressing the same phonological issues as are addressed by Allsopp, Berry, Holder and Carter.

Work on tone in other restructured Afro-English Creole language varieties has gone on. The consensus in relation to Krio is that it is tonal and tends to have one H-tone per lexical item. (Berry, 1961, 1970a, 1970b; Fyle & Jones, 1980) In addition, an H-tone is attached to the second syllables of many two-syllable items of English origin, e.g. /bebí/ "baby", /watá/ "water", /cherí/ "a kind of mango", etc. A conversion of English stress to Krio H-tone would have produced an H-tone on the first syllable. This is reminiscent of the historical UHT addition rule in GC which produced the GC cognate forms /bèebíi/, /wàatá/ and /chèríi/.

Krio employs H-tone placement in two-syllable words as a morphological device producing /bróda/ "brother" vs. /brodá/ "term of address to elder male", /sísta/ "sister" vs. /sistá/ "a nun", /kóntri/ "country" vs. /kontrí/ "a rural inhabitant", etc. (Hancock, 1977, p.166) All this looks suspiciously similar to some of the morphological functions to which tone can be put in GC, as discussed in 2.3.

Spears (1972) comes down fairly strongly in favour of some kind of tonal accent interpretation of Cayman Creole or what he refers to as Cayman Familiar. Interestingly, he has some remarks to make on the behaviour of many two-syllable items. He points out (p.128) that English stress is very often not reinterpreted as H-tone in Cayman Familiar and uses as examples /kičín/ and /čèrí/, both of which have English cognates "kitchen" and "cherry" with stress on the first syllable. We are here again probably dealing with a historical process similar to that which operated in GC. Such a process would have produced a UHT addition on to a non-initial syllable of many items which already had UHT on the first syllable.

The discussion of the status of tone in Jamaican Creole (JC) is much more unclear and controversial. (Carter, 1982; 1984; Lawton, 1963; 1971) Nevertheless, as someone with a reasonable degree of exposure to and familiarity with JC, I would venture to argue that the lexical status of the underlying high tone (UHT) is clear. Lexically assigned UHT operates in a very similar manner to the way it behaves in GC, except that tone is not put to the same wide range of morphological functions. The major difference between the two languages is at the tone group level where rules seem to operate to frequently delete non-initial UHTs in JC. It is this which partially masks the lexical role of the UHT in JC and produces so much uncertainty in the minds of some linguists studying the tonal system of the language.

All this tends to point in the direction of the view that GC is not unique amongst the phonologically restructured Afro-English Creole languages. The similarities reported between the tonal features of many of these languages are too great to be simply attributed to accident. This work has tried to provide a basis for understanding the reasons for this similarity.

REFERENCES

ALLEYNE, M, 1980, *Comparative Afro-American*, Karoma, Ann Arbor.

ALLSOPP, R., 1972, "Some suprasegmental features of Caribbean English", in *Conference on Creole Languages and Educational Development*, University of the West Indies, St. Augustine, Trinidad, July, 1972, pp.120-133.

AMAYO, A., 1980, "Tone in Nigerian English", in *Papers from the 16th Regional Meeting of the Chicago Linguistics Society*, 1980, CLS, University of Chicago, pp.1-9

ARIZA, M. de, 1980, "Stress and intonation in Haitian Creole", Paper presented to *The Conference of the Society for Caribbean Linguistics*, Aruba, 1980.

BAUM, P., 1976, "The question of decreolisation in Papiamentu phonology", in *International Journal of the Sociology of Language*, No. 7, 1976, pp.83-93.

BENDIX, E., 1983, "Sandhi phenomena in Papiamentu, African and other Creole languages", in Carrington, L. (ed.), *Studies in Caribbean Language*, Society for Caribbean Linguistics, St. Augustine, Trinidad.

BERRY, J., 1961, "English loan-words and adaptations in Sierra Leone Krio", in Le Page, R., & D. DeCamp (eds.), 1961, *Creole Language Studies II*, Macmillan, London, pp.1-6.

BERRY, J., 1970a, "A note on the prosodic structure of Krio", *International Journal of American Linguistics*, Vol. 36, No. 4, pp.266-267.

BERRY, J., 1970b, "A note on Krio tones", *African Language Studies XI*, 1970, pp.60-63.

BERRY, J., 1976, "Tone and intonation in Guyanese English", to appear in Juilland, A., (ed.), 1976 *Festchrift for Joseph H. Greenberg*, Stanford University Press, Stanford.

BIRMINGHAM, J., 1970, *The Papiamentu Language of Curacao*, PhD Thesis, University of Virginia, University Microfilms Inc., Ann Arbor, Michigan.

BOUDREAULT, M.,1970, "Le rhythme en langage Franco-Canadienne", in Leon, P. & G. Faure (eds.), 1970, *Prosodic Feature Analysis*, Librairie Didier, Montreal, pp.1-12

CARRINGTON, L., 1984, *St. Lucian Creole: A Descriptive Analysis of its Phonology and Morpho-syntax*, Helmut Buske, Hamburg.

CARTER, H., 1982, "The tonal system of Jamaican English", paper presented to *The Conference of the Society for Caribbean Linguistics*, Surinam, 1982.

CARTER, H., 1983, "How to be a tone language", in Carrington, L. (ed.), *Studies in Caribbean Language*, Society for Caribbean Linguistics, St. Augustine, Trinidad, pp.90-111.

CARTER, H., 1984, "Defining the syllable in Jamaican Creole", paper presented to *The Conference of the Society for Caribbean Linguistics*, Jamaica, 1984.

CARTER, H., 1987, "Suprasegmentals in Guyanese: some African comparisons", in Gilbert, G. (ed.), 1987, *Pidgin and Creole Languages*, University of Hawaii Press, Honolulu.

CLEMENTS, G., 1983, "The hierarchical representation of tone features", in Dihoff, I. (ed.), 1983, *Current Approaches to African Linguistics (Vol. 1)*, Foris Publications, Dordrecht, Holland.

CLEMENTS, G. & K. FORD, 1979, "Kikuyu tone shift and its synchronic consequences", *Linguistic Inquiry*, Vol. 10, No. 2, 1979, pp.179-210.

CLEMENTS, G. & S. KEYSER, 1983, *CV Phonology: A Generative Theory of the Syllable*, MIT Press, Cambridge, Massachusetts.

de CHENE, B., 1985, *The Historical Phonology of Vowel Length*, Garland Publishing Inc., New York.

EERSEL, C., 1984, "Stedman's Sranan-Notes and Queries", paper presented to *The Conference of the Society for Caribbean Linguistics*, Jamaica, 1984

FERRAZ, L., 1975, "African influence on Principense creole", *Miscelanea Luso-African*, Junta de Investigações Cientificas do Ultramar, Lisbon.

FUDGE, E., 1984, *English Word-Stress*, George Allen & Unwin, London.

FYLE, C., & E. JONES, 1980, *A Krio-English Dictionary*, Oxford University Press, Oxford.

GLOCK, N., 1972, "Role structure in Saramaccan verbs", in Grimes, J. (ed.), 1972, *Languages of the Guianas*, Summer Institute of Linguistics, Norman.

GOILO, E., 1962, *The Papiamentu Textbook*, de Wit N.V., Aruba, N.A.

GOLDSMITH, J., 1976, *Autosegmental Phonology*, Indiana University Linguistics Club. Also published in 1979 by Garland Press, New York.

HALL, R., 1948, "The Linguistic structure of Taki-Taki", *Language*, Vol. 24, No. 1, pp.92-116.

HANCOCK, I., 1977, "Lexical expansion within a closed system", in Blount, B.& M. Sanches (eds.), 1977, *Sociocultural Dimensions of Language Change*, Academic Press, New York, pp.161-171.

HARAGUCHI, S., 1977, *The Tone Pattern of Japanese: An Autosegmental Theory of Tonology*, Kaitakusha, Tokyo.

HOLDER, M., 1972, "Word accentual patterns in Guyanese English (GE) compared with British English (RP norm)", in Rigault, A. & R. Charbonneau (eds.), 1972, *Proceedings of the 7th International Congress on Phonetic Sciences, Montreal, 1971*, Mouton, The Hague, pp.897-899.

HOLDER, M., 1978, "RP & GE accentual patterns" presented to *The Conference of the Society for Caribbean Linguistics*, Barbados, 1978.

HOLDER, M., 1984, "The compound stress rule in Guyanese English", paper presented to *The Conference of the Society for Caribbean Linguistics*, Jamaica, 1984.

HUTTAR, G., 1972, "A comparative word list for Djuka", in Grimes, J. (ed.), 1972, *Languages of the Guianas*, Summer Institute of Linguistics, Norman, pp.12-21.

HUTTAR, G.& M.HUTTAR, 1972, "Notes on Djuka phonology", in Grimes, J. (ed.) 1972, *Languages of the*

Guianas, Summer Institute of Linguistics, Norman, pp.1-11.

HYMAN, L., 1975, *Phonology: Theory and Analysis*, Holt, Rinehart and Winston, New York.

HYMAN, L., 1981, "Tonal accent in Somali", *Studies in African Linguistics*, Vol. 12, No.2, 1981, pp.169-201.

HYMAN, L., 1982, "Globality and the accentual analysis of Luganda tone", *Journal of Linguistic Research*, Vol.2, No.3, 1982, pp.1-39.

HYMAN, L. & E. BYARUSHENGO, 1984, "A model of Haya tonology", in Clements, G., & J. Goldsmith (eds.), 1984, *Autosegmental Studies in Bantu Tone*, Foris Publications, Dordrecht, Holland.

HYMAN, L. & R. SCHUH, 1974, "Universals of tone rules: evidence from West Africa', *Linguistic Inquiry*, Vol. 5, No. 1, 1984, pp.81-115.

LASS, Roger, 1984, *Phonology: an introduction to basic concepts*, Cambridge University Press, New York.

LAWTON, D., 1963, *Suprasegmental Phenomena in Jamaican Creole*, Unpublished PhD dissertation, Michigan State University.

LAWTON, D., 1971, "Tone and Jamaican Creole", paper presented to *The Conference on Creole Linguistics*, Mona, Jamaica, 1971.

LEA, W., 1973, "Segmental and suprasegmental influences on fundamental frequency contours", in Hyman, L. (ed.), 1973, *Consonant Types and Tone*, Southern California Occasional Papers in Linguistics 1, pp.15-70.

LEHISTE, I., 1970, *Suprasegmentals*, MIT Press, Massachusetts.

McCAWLEY, J., 1978, "What is a tone language?", in Fromkin, V. (ed.), 1978, *Tone: A Linguistic Survey*, Academic Press, New York, pp.113-132.

MEUSSEN, A., 1970, "Tone typologies for West African languages", *African Language Studies II*, 1970, pp.266-271.

OHALA, J., 1978, "Production of tone", in Fromkin, V. (ed.), 1978, *Tone: A Linguistic Survey*, Academic Press, New York, pp.5-40.

OOMEN, A., 1981, "Gender and plurality in Rendille", *Afroasiatic Linguistics*, Vol. 8, No.1, pp.35-75.

PIKE, E., 1974, "A multiple stress system versus a tone system", *International Journal of American Linguistics*, Vol. 40, No.3, pp.169-175.

RIGAULT, A., 1970, "L'accent dans deux langages à l'accent fixe: le français et le tcheque",in Leon, P., G. Faure et al. (eds.), 1970, *Prosodic Feature Analysis*, Librairie Didier, Montreal, pp. 1-12.

ROMER, R., 1977, "Polarization phenomena in Papiamentu", *Amsterdam Creole Studies*, No. 1, 1977, pp.69-79.

ROUNTREE, S., 1972, "The phonological structure of stems in Saramaccan", in Grimes, J. (ed.), 1972, *Languages of the Guianas*, Summer Institute of Linguistics, Norman, pp.22-27.

SALAMI, A., 1972, "Vowel and consonant harmony and vowel restriction in assimilated English loan words in Yoruba", *African Language Studies*, No. 13, pp.162-181.

SCHUH, R., 1978, "Tone rules", in Fromkin, V. (ed.), 1978, *Tone: A Linguistic Survey*, Academic Press, New York, pp.221-256.

SMITH, N., 1977, "The development of the liquids in the Surinam Creoles", *Amsterdam Creole Studies*, No. 1, 1977, pp.32-54.

SPEARS, R., 1972, "Pitch and Intonation in Cayman English", in *Conference on Creole Languages and Educational Development*, University of the West Indies, St. Augustine, 1972, pp.120-133.

TAYLOR, D., 1977, *Languages of the West Indies*, John Hopkins University Press, Baltimore.

TRAILL, A., & L. FERRAZ, 1981, "The interpretation of tone in Principense Creole", *Studies in African Linguistics*, Vol. 12, No. 2, pp.205-215.

VALDMAN, A., 1978, *Le Créole: Structure, Statut et Origine*, Editions Klincksieck, Paris.

VALKOFF, M., 1966, *Studies in Portuguese and Creole* Witwatersrand University Press, Johannesburg.

VOORHOEVE, J., 1959, "An orthography for Saramaccan", *Word*, Vol. 15, pp.436-445.

VOORHOEVE, J., 1961a, "A project for the study of Creole language history" in Le Page, R., (ed.) 1961, *Creole Language Studies II* MacMillan, London, pp.99-106.

VOORHOEVE, J., 1961b, "Le ton et la grammaire dans le Saramaccan", *Word* Vol. 17, pp.146-163.

VOORHOEVE, J., 1970, "The regularity of sound correspondences in a Creole language (Sranan)", *Journal of African Languages,* Vol. 9, No.2, pp.51-69.

VOORHOEVE, J., 1973a, "Safwa as a restricted tone system", *Studies in African Languages* Vol. 4, pp.1-22.

VOORHOEVE, J., 1973b, "Historical and linguistic evidence in favour of the relaxation theory in the formation of Creoles", *Language in Society,* Vol. 2, pp.133-145.

Index

Accent 6, 7, 10, 13, 24, 40, 87
  stress 6, 7, 10, 13-6, 19, 23-4, 27-9, 32-6, 40, 46, 48, 62, 65-7, 69, 72, 86
  tonal 19, 22, 24, 39, 66-7, 69, 81, 85-6, 132, 135
Akan 80
Assimilation 21-3, 24, 26, 120
Autosegmental Phonology 21

Bantu 7, 12, 15, 18, 19
  Eastern 11, 22-3
  Proto 7

Chinese 11, 116
Compound Words 48-9, 51-3, 65, 96, 111, 133
  tone in 52, 55, 65
Consonants 27, 28, 30, 32, 34, 36, 44, 61, 79-80, 127-8
  clusters 27-9, 31-2, 36-7, 42, 44, 77
  inter-vocalic Deletion 7, 69, 74, 81-2
Creole Languages
  Afro-English 24, 66, 72-4, 96, 130, 134-5
  Afro-European 6-9, 18-9, 21-2, 24, 35, 39, 48, 55, 57, 61, 64, 69, 70, 72
  Afro-Iberian 63
  Afro-French 70
  Afro-Portuguese 66
  Afro-Spanish 66
  Barbadian 6
  Cayman 6, 135
  Djuka 6, 8, 12, 24-31, 33-4, 41,8, 54-5, 66-9, 72-6, 79-83, 93, 96
  Guyanese 3, 6-7, 72, 130, 133
  Haitian 70
  Jamaican 6, 135
  Papiamentu 55-65, 69-70
  Principense 8, 34-41, 43, 45-6, 67, 69

Proto Afro-English 73
Proto Creole Languages 19, 20
Proto Guyanese 73-6, 79, 82-4, 86, 93, 95, 105, 118, 132
St. Lucian 70
Saramaccan Plantation 6, 12, 24-7, 30, 32, 48-52, 54-5, 66, 69, 72-4, 79, 80, 96,
Sierra Leone   See Krio
Sranan 24-28, 30-4, 37, 39-40, 44, 46, 66-7, 69, 96
Surinam Plantation 29-31, 33-34, 41, 66, 69

Digo 23
Dissimilation 16, 23-4
Downdrift 10, 119-120, 123-5, 127-8, 132-3
Downstep 119, 123-7, 129, 132
Dutch 28, 30, 32, 34, 43-4, 48, 55

Edo 17-8, 22
English
  American 6
  British 6, 19, 133
  Guyanese 133
  Nigerian 16-21
Epenthesis 38

French 70

Greek, Classical 85

Hausa 17-8
Haya 23

Igbo 18, 21-2, 24
Ijo 19
Intensity 10, 12-3, 33, 35, 37, 46, 48, 59
Intonation 70, 119, 120, 127-8, 132

Japanese 21, 80-1, 85-6

Kikuyu 21-2
Krio 6, 69, 134
Kwa 14, 18-9

Language Contact 6, 13, 15, 18-9, 25, 37, 63, 65-6, 71-2
Length
 vowel 10, 15, 35, 37, 59-60, 75, 85, 134
Lithuanian 80
Loudness See Intensity
Luganda 22-3

Mande Languages 18-9
Mora Prominence 7-8, 12, 85, 105-6

Niger-Congo Languages 18, 20-1, 48, 72
Nigerian Pidgin English 16-21

Phonological Restructuring 6, 130
Phrase Level Tone 19, 119
Pidgin 20
Pitch 6, 9-12, 14, 21, 23, 33, 35, 39-41, 46, 60, 60, 62, 67, 69-70, 80, 84-5, 119-128, 130,
Pitch Accent 22, 24, 132
Portuguese 6, 13, 19, 25-6, 34-40, 44, 55-6, 63, 65, 67, 69
Prominence 7, 12, 33, 35, 39, 40-1, 45, 67, 105-6
 stress 8, 33-4, 45-6, 67, 69-70, 84-5

 tonal 8, 12, 13, 24, 34, 45-6, 48, 50, 67, 69-70, 85

Safwa 12-3, 24
Saramaccan See Creole Lang.
Sentence Level Tone 47, 53-4, 119-127, 129
Shona 12, 15
Somali 24, 67, 85-6
Spanish 55-6, 63, 65-6, 70
Stress
 definition 43
 foot 42-3, 45-50, 54
 placement 48, 55, 58, 70, 107, 133,
 reduction 11, 83
 reinterpretation 86, 88, 90-1
Substratum 6
Surinam 24-8, 66

Syllable 6, 9-10
 conflation 7-8, 81
 nucleus 78-82, 84-6, 89, 121
 restructuring 8, 28, 32, 34, 69, 82, 85-6, 88, 105
 stressed 8-16, 19, 23, 29-41, 43, 45-6, 48-9, 54-6, 58-9, 63-5, 81-4, 91, 130-1
 structure 12, 27-8, 34-5, 37-8, 40, 42, 44, 70, 72, 75
 weight 12, 29, 80
Syncope 32, 81-2

Tonal Morphology 96, 104
Tone
 assimilation 8, 16, 20, 22-4, 32, 40, 44, 119-20
 copying 22-3, 29, 32, 41, 46-7, 52-4, 83, 120-1, 123
 definition 8
 deletion 53-4, 63, 94, 111, 113, 118, 120, 135
 dissimilation 16, 23-4
 domain of 90-1
 lexical Specification of 9, 11, 18, 20, 29, 39, 60, 70-1, 80, 86-7, 104, 114-5, 117-8
 polarisation 55
 rules 16-8, 20-4, 32-3, 40-2, 47-8, 51, 53, 56, 66, 110-2, 114, 118, 133, 135
 shift 21, 27-9, 46, 48, 67
 underlying 8, 17-24, 29-35, 40-3, 45-58, 60-71, 80-90, 120-1, 123, 133, 135
 verbal 60, 65, 111
Tonga 11, 22, 84
Tonification 24, 48
 incomplete 7-8, 21-3, 32, 34-5, 41, 45, 47, 66-7, 69-70
Typology of Tonal Systems 8-9

Vowel(s) 7, 12-4, 16, 22, 27, 29
 as bearer of tone 9, 28-9, 34, 37-40, 42, 46, 49, 55
 deletion 28, 30-4, 40, 44, 54, 69, 74-5, 86
 height 73-5
 prominence 13, 35, 39-40, 45, 48, 67
 reduction 10